# 目次

725
.210973
.T34
1996

AEE0389

# CONTENTS

ART DIRECTOR : YASUHIKO TAGUCHI／TAGUCHI DESIGN

# 時代の流れを反映した新しいショッピングセンターの動き

田口泰彦

順調な伸びを示していたアメリカのショッピングセンターの新規建設は，1990年代初頭の2年間に激減した。

リセッション（景気後退）の影響で，アンカーテナントである百貨店の不振もあり，不調が続いたこの業界も，90年代中頃からやっと回復してきたが，その中でショッピングセンターが新しい顔を見せ始めた。

不景気の中，価格に敏感な消費者のニーズに応えた各種の大型店，トイザラス（玩具／子供用品），ホーム・デポ（家の修繕用品），サーキット・シティー（家電），バーンズ＆ノーブル（本／レコード）などのようなチェーンのスーパーストアや，一流ブランド品を安く販売するアウトレットモールなどが4〜5年の間に急成長し，流通業態に大きな変化が現れた。

共稼ぎ夫婦の増加などによる，自分の時間を大事にするライフスタイルの変化は，TVショッピングやコンピューターショッピング，カタログショッピングでほとんどの物が手に入る生活を可能にした。

消費者が，自分のニーズに合ったショッピングの仕方ができる時代となり，彼らの買い物パターンも大きく変わってきている。

情報化時代の消費者ニーズにどのように応えるか，ショッピングセンターが新しい時代を迎えたとも言える。

ショッピングセンターは，数の上で飽和状態に近い。パワーセンター，アウトレットセンターなど，新しい業態の進出でマーケットというパイは小さくなりつつある。ショッピングセンターは，自分のマーケットは何か（ポジショニング），顧客のニーズの的確な把握と，各種アメニティー，サービスなどの充実によって，消費者にアピールする施設を作らなければならない。

マーケットニーズにどのように応えるか，アメリカはマーケットリサーチが大変発達しているが，1996年8月にオープンした「サマーセット・コレクション・ノース」（本書には「サマーセット・コレクション」を集録）は，顧客のニーズをセンターのデザインからテナント構成にまで反映させるため，広範囲なマーケットリサーチを行っている。

デトロイト郊外のこのアップスケール・センターは，既存の「サマーセット・コレクション」の拡張であり，ハイウエーに架けた陸橋で結ばれている。買い物客はセンターの表玄関で車を降り，帰りは反対側の玄関で車をピックアップするコンピューター化したバレーパーキングを持つ。SC内には化粧品の大手エスティー・ローダーのスパ（約557㎡）があり，幅2.4mだった通路は5.4mに拡幅され，2階へのアクセスを良くし，休息のためのベンチを多く設置するなど，細部にわたって顧客のニーズに応え，マーケット内における地位の確立を図った。

社会環境，流通環境の変化によって，ショッピングセンターも新しい役割と変化が見られるようになった。

## エンターテインメント化

今ほとんどのショッピングセンターにあるフードコートは，80年代に買い物と食事の楽しみを結びつける，アメニティーの重要な要素として登場した。映画館やライブ・ミュージックのあるレストラン，ナイトスポット，ミュージアム，あるいは回転木馬などのアミューズメント・パークの一部がショッピングセンターの中に作られ，買い物＋αの楽しさが付け加えられた。

また楽しく買い物できる環境づくりとして，ショッピングセンターのデザインにおいてもスカイライトの多用や，池，木，観葉植物によって屋内に屋外環境を提供したり，非日常的なファンタジーのあるイメージ空間が作られた。

ローマ時代の町並みがドラマチックなラスベガスの「フォーラム・ショップス」，ロサンゼルスの街を凝縮して店のファサードが作られたユニバーサル・スタジオの「シティーウオーク」など，観光スポットでもある。

## コミュニティーセンター化

郊外に発展した居住コミュニティー，サテライト・オフィス街など，都心部から離れた場所に人口が移動し，それに伴ってショッピングセ

ンターも作られてきた。

郊外に住む人々にとって町の中心というものが無く，コミュニティーの連帯感も薄いことから，近年，地域の核，または新しいタウンセンターとしての役割がショッピングセンターの中に取り入れられるようになった。各種イベントの開催，集会所の提供などを通じ，コミュニティーの社交の場となっている。

日常的な用事が買い物しながら済ませられるように郵便局，図書館，運転免許証の交付所，警察署，自治体の事務所などがショッピングセンターに置かれることも多くなった。

このようなショッピングセンターの敷地に隣接して，老人用や公共アパートが建てられ，そこに住む人々が，車が無くても買い物や日常の用事が済ませられるタウンセンターも出現している。

フロリダ州タンパの「ブランドン・タウンセンター」は，コミュニティーの核，タウンセンターとしての機能を持ちながら，またパワーセンターを敷地内に作ることによってワンストップ・ショッピングセンターとなっている。

### ワンストップ／巨大化

集客性，マーケット・ニーズを反映したパワーセンターを同じ敷地内に作る，「ワンストップ・ショッピング」のコンセプトによる新しいショッピングセンターも増えている。

前出の「ブランドン・タウンセンター」の，自然環境を考慮して，美しくランドスケープされた敷地内にはパワーセンターがある。サービス，マーチャンダイズ（カタログストア），ターゲット（ディスカウンター），ブロック・バスター・ミュージック，トイザラス，バーンズ＆ノーブルなどのスーパーストアがあり，新しいショッピングセンターの必要条件（役割）をすべて満たして作られている。

巨大化するショッピングモールにおいて，忙しい買い物客が効率良くショッピングできるよう商品（テナント）ごとにグループ化したのが，マサチューセッツ州ナティックの「ナティック・モール」。「今日

はこのセクションで買い物し，週末は同じショッピングセンター内の別のセクションで買い物する」というアイデアで改装された。

### 高級化

他のショッピングセンターとの差別化の方法はいろいろあるが，カントリークラブ・タイプも増えてきている。

大きな商圏には，高所得者をターゲットとして，隣接センターとの差別化を図った高級ショッピングセンターがある。

ゆったりとした豪華なインテリアに一流テナントが入り，高級ホテルを思わせるようなラウンジで，全体にエレガントに作られている。フードコートは無く，フルサービスのレストランがそれに代わる。アトランタの「フィップス・プラザ」，セントルイスの「プラザ・フロンテナック」などがその典型と言えよう。

四角い箱のような，コンクリートで無表情の，まわりの環境になじまないショッピングセンターの建物が，周囲のスケールや環境に調和し，温かみのある建物としてデザインされるようになった。インテリアも安らぎを感じる，あるいはエキサイトメントを感じる楽しい空間づくりがなされている。

特に古くなったショッピングセンターのリノベーションにおいては，建物の入り口など外部から見てもっとも効果的にその結果が現れる場所や，買い物客が一番目に止めやすいセンターコート／広場などが主な対象になっている。さらに大掛かりなリノベーションでは，マーケットに合わせてテナントを変えたり，コミュニティーの場を導入，エンターテインメント／アミューズメント性のある施設を加えることにより消費者ニーズ／新しい役割に対応した新しいショッピングセンターのイメージづくりをしている。

どのような流通業態が出てこようとも，変化する消費者のニーズをとらえ，マーケットに合った施設が作られる限り，われわれにとってショッピングセンターは，わざわざ足を運んで，訪れて楽しい場所なのである。

# New Movement in American Shopping Centers

YASUHIKO TAGUCHI

The number of new shopping center projects has declined sharply in the first two years of the 1990s. Building new shopping centers appears to be a thing of the past.

The recent recession made anchor tenants, or departmentstores, so slack that they have to be altered to regain lost ground during the end of the 1990s. However, various large-scale stores, which are susceptible to the customers' changing needs, have been growing during the past four to five years. Super stores like Toys-R-Us, The Home Depot, Circuit City, Barnes & Noble, and outlet centers have brought drastic change in distribution systems.

The lifestyle for those families with two working parents who value their own time, have shifted. They have been shown to shop and purchase almost any kinds of goods, through a variety of shopping styles, such as T.V. shopping, on-line shopping, catalog shopping, and others. The numerous needs of the consumers are mostly met by these suitable shopping techniques. A new era for shopping centers has developed in which they have meet the demands of this age to survive.

There is nearly no more space for ordinary shopping centers. Their market is being threatened by power centers, outlet centers, and other new types of commercial facilities. Shopping centers now have to take under consideration of their positions, targets, and needs to improve their amenity and services.

Needless to say, the market research in the United States has been developed and used effectively. There is a good example of such market research in Somerset Collection North, which depends on a comprehensive market research to design a mall to respond to their customer's needs. This upscale center, in the suburb of Detroit, is annexed to the Somerset Collection main building by a bridge. It has computerized valet parking by which shoppers get out of their cars at the front of the mall and retrieve them after they have finished shopping. There is a spa facility by Estee Lauder (557 square meters) and also a wide walkway (2.4 meters wide and 5.4 meters long), and an easy and smooth access to the second floor. A number of rest areas were also built with benches for the customers. They are parts of the tactics used to help this mall position itself in the market.

With changes in the social environment and distributions systems, shopping centers appear to face a serious phenomenal shift of this age.

Shopping Malls as an Entertainment Facility Today, most shopping centers have food courts, which were born in the 1980s as an important convenience combining shopping and dining. To display added value to visitors, shopping centers now have movie theaters, live music stages, museums, and merry-go-rounds.

The design of shopping centers has also changed very much to create a more fun place to shop. They now use a lot of skylights, artificial ponds, plants, ornamental flowers, and trees. The aim is to create an outdoor feeling or space like that of a fantasy. The dramatic Ancient Roman townscape of the Forum in Las Vegas and outlook of a miniaturized streetscape of Los Angeles in Universal Studio's City Walk are very popular tourist spots.

### Shopping Centers as Community Centers

Shopping centers have been built close to residential communities, satellite offices, in accordance with the movement of population from the inner city since the 1950s. Suburbs without a core in their town have little community consciousness. Therefore they welcome a kind of community center or town center which is designed as a key amenity of the shopping center. Where they can enjoy various events and use the public plaza as a gathering place of the community. The shopping centers can also function to provide the consumer's daily conveniences. They can shop and run errands at their local government offices, post office, library, police station, or even the driver's license office. Next to such convenient shopping centers, public residential areas were built for aged and retired people so that they can shop and accomplish their needs without the use of cars.

Brandon Town Center in Tampa, Florida is a shopping center which makes up the core of the town center. In addition a power center will also be built in the same site making it a one-stop shopping center.

## One-Stop Shopping Centers at Grand Scale

A number of shopping centers are being built with large a so-called power center based upon a concept of " one-stop shopping " recently. The Brandon Town Center, mentioned earlier, with its power center was built with a beautiful landscaped compound which reflected its natural environment. The power center has a Service Merchandise catalog store, a Target discount store, a Blockbuster Music store, a Toys-R-Us toy store, a Barnes & Noble book store, and other stores. It definitely fits the definition of these new shopping centers. In huge shopping malls, it is necessary to divide the mall into sections. Since the mall is so huge in these days, customers can visit each section at a time to meet their shopping needs. This is the case in the Natick Mall of Natick, Massachusetts. The visitors can shop efficiently without having to shop every inch of the mall.

## High-ended Shopping Centers

There are many specific differences exhibited among shopping centers to compete with each other. Recently the country club type shopping centers have emerged and are increasing. These shopping centers were built to accommodate those classy high income customers who are looking for malls with more of an edge. Up-scale tenants occupy the stores and create an environment much like a hotel lounge. The malls are roomy and relaxing with gorgeous interior decorations. It has no food court, but instead has full-service restaurants. Among such places are Phipps Plaza in Atlanta and Plaza Frontenac in St. Louis.

Shopping centers that are built like a concrete shaped box often do not fit their surroundings without any character. Recent shopping centers are designed on a human scale to be in harmony with the rest of the neighborhood.

They are built with friendly interiors that make the customer feel comfortable and enjoyable.

The effective way to renovate old shopping centers is to design the areas, such as the main entrance in addition to the food courts and public plazas, which are more noticeable to the customer. In large scale renovations, the developers tend to change tenants, in accordance with the changing market. It also adds the community center of a new type, entertainment, and other amusing types of facilities to respond to the customers' needs. Thus it creates a new image in response to a new role of the shopping center. Visiting a shopping center can be a very enjoyable experience as long as it satisfies the customer's needs and is challenged to create a better shopping environment that can keep up with the changing market.

# 作品リスト／LIST

**WEST**

❶ ユニバーサルシティウォーク
建築デザイン／ジャーディ・パートナーシップ
UNIVERSAL CITYWALK
ARCHITECT : THE JERDE PARTNERSHIP

❷ ダウンタウン プラザ
建築デザイン／ジャーディ・パートナーシップ
DOWNTOWN PLAZA
ARCHITECT : THE JERDE PARTNERSHIP

❸ トライアングル・スクエア
建築デザイン／アルツーン&ポーター・アーキテクツ
TRIANGLE SQUARE
ARCHITECT : ALTOON & PORTER ARCHITECTS

❹ グレート モール オブ ザ ベイエリア
建築デザイン／ワー・ウィー&アソシエート
GREAT MALL OF THE BAY AREA
ARCHITECT : WAH YEE & ASSOCIATES

❺ バレンシア タウンセンター
建築デザイン／RTKLアソシエイツ
VALENCIA TOWN CENTER
ARCHITECT : RTKL ASSOCIATES

❻ カフマヌ・センター
建築デザイン／アルツーン&ポーター アーキテクツ
KAAHUMANU CENTER
ARCHITECT : ALTOON & PORTER ARCHITECTS

❼ アロハ・タワー・マーケットプレイス
建築デザイン／ダゴスティノ イゾ カーク アーキテクツ
ALOHA TOWER MARKETPLACE
ARCHITECT : D'AGOSTINO IZZO QUIRK ARCHITECTS

**SORTHWEST**

❽ ウッドランド モール
建築デザイン／エルバサーニ&ローガン アーキテクト
WOODLANDS MALL
ARCHITECT : ELBASANI & LOGAN ARCHITECTS

❾ メーンストリート
建築デザイン／パルマー ブルック スクーリー
MAIN STREET
ARCHITECT : PALMER BROOK SCHOOLEY

❿ レイクライン・モール
建築デザイン／ウイリアム グレイブス アーキテクツ
LAKELINE MALL
ARCHITECT : WILLIAM GRAVES ARCHITECTS

**NORTHEAST**

⓫ シカゴ プレイス
建築デザイン／スキッドモア・オーウイングス&メリル
CHICAGO PLACE
ARCHITECT : SKIDMORE, OWINGS & MERRILL

⓬ 900 ノース・ミシガン
建築デザイン／パーキンズ&ウィル+コーン・ペダーセン・フォックス
900 NORTH MICHIGAN
ARCHITECT : PERKINS & WILL, KOHN PEDERSEN FOX ASSOCIATES

⓭ サマーセット・コレクション
建築デザイン／JPRAアーキテクツ
THE SOMERSET COLLECTION
ARCHITECT : JPRA ARCHITECTS

⓮ ネービー・ピア
建築デザイン／VOAアソシエイツ, ベンジャミン トンプソン アソシエイツ
NAVY PIER
ARCHITECT : VOA ASSOCIATES, BENJAMIN THOMPSON ASSOCIATES

⓯ タワー シティー センター
建築デザイン／RTKLアソシエイツ
TOWER CITY CENTER
ARCHITECT : RTKL ASSOCIATES

⓰ クリーブランド アーケード
建築デザイン／カプラン・マクロフリン・ディアズ アーキテクツ
CLEVELAND ARCADE
ARCHITECT : KAPLAN, McLAUGHLIN, DIAZ

⓱ セントルイス・ギャラリア
建築デザイン／ヘルムス, オバタ&カサバウム社
SAINT LOUIS GALLERIA
ARCHITECT : HELLMUTH, OBATA & KASSABAUM

⓲ プラザ・フロンテナック
建築デザイン／ヘルムス, オバタ&カサバウム社
PLAZA FRONTENAC
ARCHITECT : HELLMUTH, OBATA & KASSABAUM

⓳ ルーズベルト・フィールド
建築デザイン／RTKLアソシエイツ
ROOSEVELT FIELD
ARCHITECT : RTKL ASSOCIATES

⓴ ショップズ・アト・プルデンシャルセンター
建築デザイン／シクス ジェニングス ケリ・ブリュワー事務所
THE SHOPS AT PRUDENTIAL CENTER
ARCHITECT : SIKES JENNINGS KELLY & BREWER

㉑ ケンブリッジサイド・ギャラリア
建築デザイン／アローストリート事務所
CAMBRIDGESIDE GALLERIA
ARCHITECT : ARROWSTREET

㉒ ナティック・モール
建築デザイン／アローストリート事務所
NATICK MALL
ARCHITECT : ARROWSTREET

**SOUTHEAST**

㉓ フィップス・プラザ
建築デザイン／トンプソン・ベンチュレット・スタインバック社
PHIPPS PLAZA
ARCHITECT : THOMPSON, VENTULLET, STAINBACK & ASSOCIATES

㉔ ノースポイントモール
建築デザイン／エルバサーニ&ローガン・アーキテクツ
NORTH POINT MALL
ARCHITECT : ELBASANI & LOGAN ARCHITECTS

㉕ マイツナー・パーク
建築デザイン／クーパー・ケリー事務所
MIZNER PARK
ARCHITECT : COOPER CARRY & ASSOCIATES

㉖ ブロワード・モール
建築デザイン／FRCHデザイン・ワールド・ワイド
BROWARD MALL
ARCHITECT : FRCH DESIGN WORLD WIDE

㉗ ブランドン・タウンセンター
建築デザイン／RTKLアソシエイツ
BRANDON TOWNCENTER
ARCHITECT : RTKL ASSOCIATES

㉘ ユニバーシティー モール
建築デザイン／アンソニー・ベルーチ・アーキテクツ
UNIVERSITY MALL
ARCHITECT : ANTHONY BELLUSCHI ARCHITECTS

㉙ ローマンズ・ファッション・アイランド
建築デザイン／ジョン R.ディベロ アーキテクト
LOEHMANN'S FASHION ISLAND
ARCHITECT : JOHN R.DEBELLO ARCHITECT

㉚ ペムブローク・レーク・モール
建築デザイン／スピリス キャンデラ&パートナーズ
PEMBROKE LAKES MALL
ARCHITECT : SPILLIS CANDELA & PARTNERS

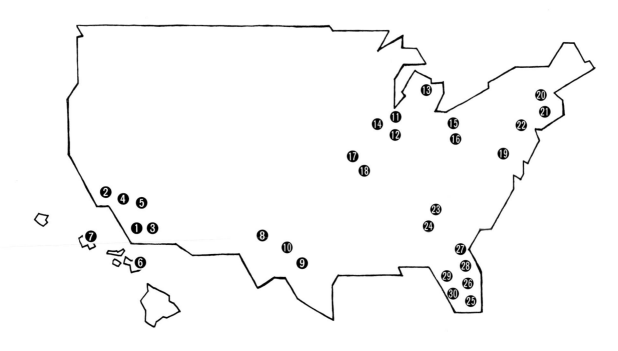

# UNIVERSAL CITYWALK

## ARCHITECT : THE JERDE PARTNERSHIP

Los Angeles, California

1

2

3

1. View of Center Court
2. View of West Walk
3. View of West Walk
4. View of West Walk at Night
5. West Walk Entrance
6. 7. 8. 9. 10. 11. Storefront

4

5

6

7

8

9

10

11

Universal CityWalk is a unique mixed-use pedestrian promenade which opened in May of 1993, nearly 80 years after the grand opening of Universal Studios.

Adjoining the Universal Studios Hollywood theme park, the 6,200 seat Universal Amphitheater, and the 18 screen Universal City Cineplex Cinemas, CityWalk is a four-block long mosaic of Southern California's outstanding cultural, culinary, entertainment, retail and architectural amenities. The result is a fun "people place" that brings forth the beast of what Los Angeles is known for.

Universal CityWalk is an urban village community of the future. With its dome shaped roofline, the village actually follow the natural hill form. The selected taller buildings penetrate the memorable low-rise silhouette in areas designated to have minimal imapact on neighboring residents. An eclectic assortment of more than 3 dozens facades which house casual dining restaurants, magic club／dinner theatre; various specialty food and refreshment establishments, retail shops, cinematic thrill ride and neon art museum. Consists of three segments : 1) The East Walk near the entrance to the Universal City Cinemas; East side entrance has stadium size video message screen to Universal CityWalk to the Lighthouse Bar on real sand beach near

12. View of Center Court
13. View of Center Court
14. View of Center Court

Glandstone's Restaurant. 2) Center Court with dramatic open-air space frame dome. 3) West Walk near Universal Studio Hollywood tour. West end has mega-size surfboard atop the Current Wave clothing store. Series of flowers, vines and ivies adorn the wall of the Center Court providing a season change in color and shapes. Throughout array of awnings, trellises, canopies and trees will create pleasant shady areas. Nightfall comes alive with crackle tube neon cove and accent lighting, towers with theatrical lighting and light refracting panels which deflect splashes of color throughout the plazas.

12

13

14

15. Dining in Wizardz
16. Fountain at Center Court
17. Fountain at Center Court

15

16

17

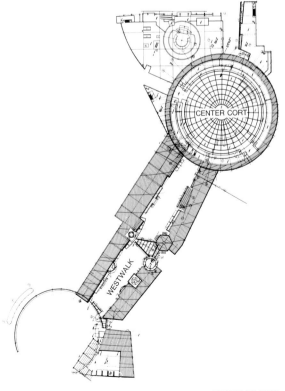

ROOF PLAN 1:2500

18. Dining in Gladstones
19. Gladstones
20. Lighthouse Beach
21. Scale Model

18

19

20

## GLADSTONES Seafood Restaurant

Design carries through images of LA coast as it was, along with real pieces of history. The 706 seat restaurnat uses 1901 battleship buoy, recycled wood frame from USS Bon Homme Richard and the hostess desk is an outboard motor from a barge turned upside down. Also on premise is Morisawa which serves sushi & tempura. Outdoor patio sit atop real sand beach. To complete the coastal image is an 80 foot lighthouse.

GLADSTONES
Owner : Robert J. Morris Enterprises
Designer : Sam Lopata Inc.
Photos : Richard Rownak

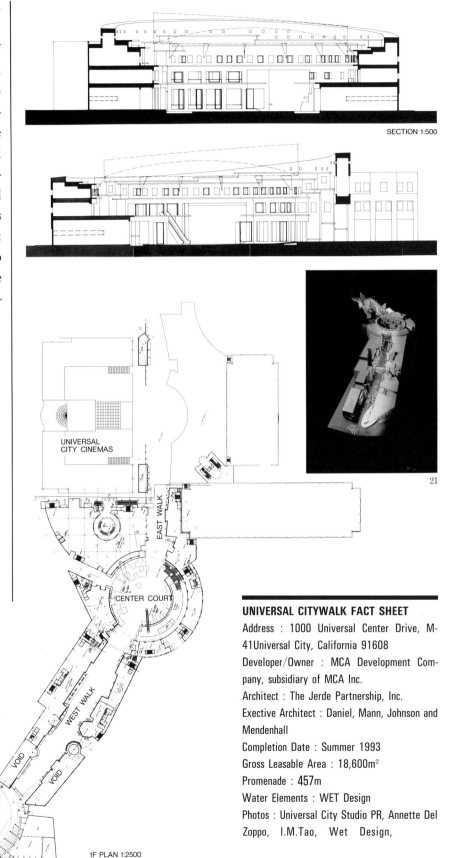

SECTION 1:500

21

UNIVERSAL
CITY CINEMAS

EAST WALK

CENTER COURT

WEST WALK

VOID

VOID

1F PLAN 1:2500

### UNIVERSAL CITYWALK FACT SHEET
Address : 1000 Universal Center Drive, M-41Universal City, California 91608
Developer/Owner : MCA Development Company, subsidiary of MCA Inc.
Architect : The Jerde Partnership, Inc.
Exective Architect : Daniel, Mann, Johnson and Mendenhall
Completion Date : Summer 1993
Gross Leasable Area : 18,600m$^2$
Promenade : 457m
Water Elements : WET Design
Photos : Universal City Studio PR, Annette Del Zoppo, I.M.Tao, Wet Design,

Jon Jerde

**INTERVIEW :** Design Process with Jon Jerde, Jerde Partnership. How did you approach the design for Universal CityWalk? On every project, I set up the spirit of it and the design intentions. Over the years, we've been deeply committed to the idea of designing the ultimate communal enclaves. We think of it as designing the experiences rather than the buildings; designing all the things that happen to you. What was your biggest challenge?

It was to deliver a city that Universal never had. It is very timely in that LA has always had an identity crisis. LA isn't a great megalopolis but a series of nested villages. Westwood, East LA, Hollywood, West Hollywood, Encino-these are really neighborhoods that are known by their own inhabitants. And they are building block of identity for people. How did you make CityWalk a reflection of LA? We made a study of all the great things about LA which tended to be kind of anonymous architecture. It was the quieter buildings on Beverly, Melrose, Sunset Blvd, occasionally was this intriguing LA kind of place. So we digested all those parts and re-conceived it in terms of the language of the architecture of the street system of Universal

CityWalk. How will your architecture affect visitors? Universal CityWalk is an enclave for people to get together and hoot it up. On foot, Los Angeles has never been a communal city. It's been this great collection of backyards. Some parts of the city like the 3rd Street Promenade, Melrose, Sunset Strip and Venice Main Street have spontaneously gone communal. Here, we're hoping to create one intentionally where people can come together, be safe, be on the street and do multiple things. It's safer here because it's on private property. What makes the building facades so distinctive? It builds on the idea that no theme is the theme, buildings alone aren't the issue. It's everything including what's

layered on-murals that get painted on, signages that go on-become an ultimate of a LA street. Can you describe the "Layering" concept? What we discovered looking at the streets of LA was that they were as much made up of the background texture but they were also as much made up of the layers that get added on by the tenants who come in to inhabit those buildings. Sometimes buildings have residuals of many inhabitants that come into them. Each leaves something of their own. So those layers continue to grow and add to an entire atmosphere that gets layered onto a building. And so, it has this kind of hybrid that continues to happen.

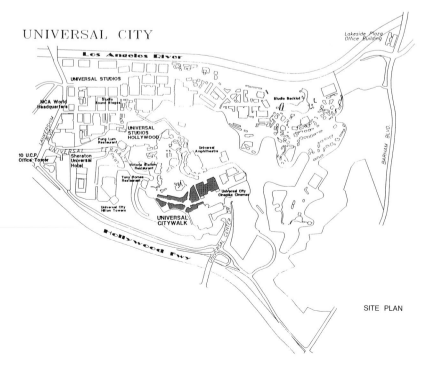

SITE PLAN

# DOWNTOWN PLAZA

## ARCHITECT : THE JERDE PARTNERSHIP

Sacramento, California

1

Against the outward growth of suburbs, the downtown shops had to unite and redevelop the traditional downtown. The renovation and extension of Downtown Plaza, a joint venture between Hahn Development of San Diego and Downtown Plaza Associates was a result of one such counter measure. Downtown Plaza is made up of four buildings : Piazza, Fifth Street Market, Rotunda and Garden Court. Piazza is an open-air two floor situated near the renewed Macy's and seven screen UA cinema complex. Visitors on the second floor enjoy their meals while looking down onto the courtyard below. A beautiful access way connect the Plaza with Old Sacramento. Fifth Street Market is comprised of small shops and kiosks, creating a bazaar-like atmosphere. Rotunda is modeled after the State Capital with 25 meter high dome. Laser shows can be seen nightly. Garden Court was built to provide shoppers a space for entertainment and events. Most of the original downtown shops and renovated Weinstock's are located between here and the Rotunda for shoppers' convenience. Also added are artistic, larger than life statues and a fountain decorated with handmade tiles. America Live and 7 screen UA cinema offer the key entertainment.

1. East Entrance
2. Garden Court
3. Clock Tower
4. View of Plaza
5. Plaza at Night

2

3

4

5

6. View of Garden Court

7. Passageway

8. Rotunda

9. View of Fifth Street Market

6

7

8

10. Looking from Plaza at Fifth Street Market
11. Signboard
12. Directory
13. Sculpture

10

11

12

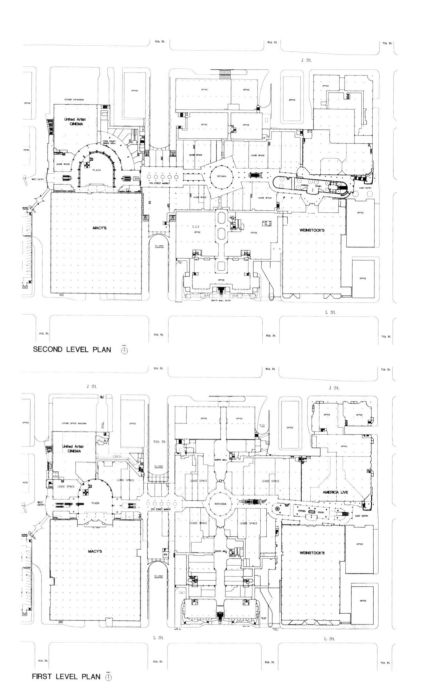

SECOND LEVEL PLAN

FIRST LEVEL PLAN

**DOWNTOWN PLAZA FACT SHEET**

Address : 547 L Street, Sacramento, California 95814

13

Developer/Owner : Downtown Plaza Associates, Hahn Corporation

America Live : Harboragel, Ltd.

Architect/Interior Design : The Jerde Partnership Inc.

Renovation Date : October 1993

Gross Size of Center : 133,000m²

Anchor/Key Tenant : Macy's(36,950m²), Weinstock's(19,000m²)

Number of Parking Spaces : 4,000

Total Cost of Construction : 157million $

Photos : I.M.Tao, Ken Uwabo

14. Food Court
15. Food Court
16. Game Keeper
17. Cafeteria
18. Kiosk

14

17

15

16

18

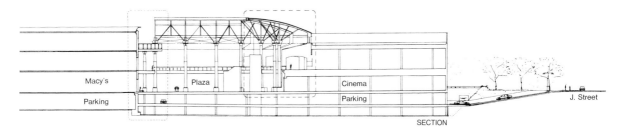

Macy's    Plaza    Cinema    J. Street

Parking    Parking

SECTION

19. America Live
20. America Live
21. America Live

19

## America Live

America Live has a maximum capacity of 6,000. It is composed of nine sections : a comedy club, a computer game complex, 2 restaurants, 2 theme discos, 2 night clubs and a sports bar. All these facilities provide dining.

20

21

America Live carefully manages this one-stop, amusement "adult Disneyland" in numerous shopping centers throughout the USA.

# TRIANGLE SQUARE

## ARCHITECT : ALTOON & PORTER ARCHITECTS

Costa Mesa, California

1

2

1. Niketown Facade
2. Facade
3. Town Square Gate
4. Newport Boulevard Entrance
5. Town Square Entrance
6. Gap Entrance

3

4

5

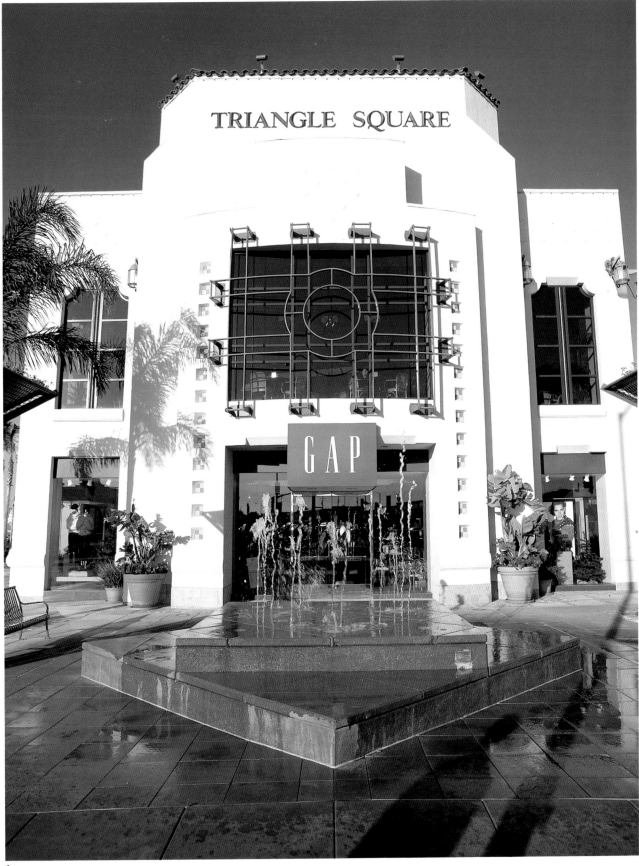

7. View of Town Square
8. View of Town Square
9. View of Town Square

8

9

Located in one of the busiest intersections in Orange County, this power entertainment center opened with 98% occupancy in May 1993, during the recession. Contrary to the norm, the 18,000 sq. meter retail area is built around a nine story central parking structure. Anchor stores are Niketown, Virgin Megastore, Gap, Barnes & Noble Bookstore, 8 screen movie theater and a supermarket. To counter its relative small site, the strategy was to bring in major labels. 2,900 square meter Niketown opened its third store in the USA. Virgin Megastore is its second and the 1,160 sq. meter Gap is the largest of its chain.

The design team took advantage of the site's unique triangular shape and built the entrances facing out to the street. The multi-level, Mediterranean style complex has three levels. Supermarket is located underground. The retail spaces on the street level is designed to harmonize with the neighboring environment. Restaurants, movie theater and other entertainment facilities are located on the second level. The open air Town Square is provided to street performers, local charity and holiday events.

10. View of Escalator Space
11. 12. Street Bench
13. View of Promenade
14. Rest Area at Town Square

10

11

12

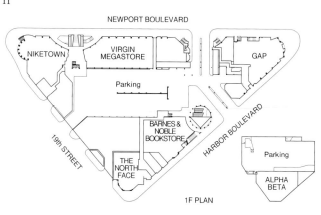

NEWPORT BOULEVARD

NIKETOWN
VIRGIN MEGASTORE
GAP
Parking
BARNES & NOBLE BOOKSTORE
THE NORTH FACE
Parking
ALPHA BETA
19th STREET
HARBOR BOULEVARD

1F PLAN

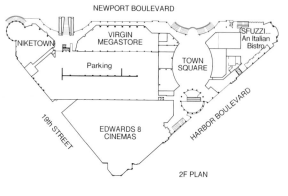

NEWPORT BOULEVARD

NIKETOWN
VIRGIN MEGASTORE
SFUZZI... An Italian Bistro
Parking
TOWN SQUARE
EDWARDS 8 CINEMAS
19th STREET
HARBOR BOULEVARD

2F PLAN

It serves as a center for local community activities. To create 62,000 sq. meters of total floor space (44,000 parking and 18,000 retail sq. meters) on a mere 18,000 sq. meters was a design victory. Entry access is available from all three streets surrounding the complex. Each megastores provide its own unique landmark. For example, the illuminated dome of Niketown is visible from the freeway, Virgin Megastore has 186 sq. meter storefront, and Mediterranean style Gap is located where Newport Blvd. meets Harbor Blvd.

15. Virgin Megastore
16. Niketown
17. Candystore and Restaurant

15

16

17

**TRIANGLE SQUARE FACT SHEET**
Address : 1870 B-002 Harbor Blvd., Costa
Mesa, California
Owner : Triangle Square Joint Venture
Architect : Altoon & Porter Architects
Completion Date : May 1993
Total Area of Site : 18,000m²
Gross Size of Center : 62,000m²
Key Tenant : Alpha Beta Super Market(4,
000m²), Niketown(2,900m²), Virgin Megastor-
e(2,510m²), Gap(1,160m²)
Photos : Ken Uwabo, Koichiro Hayashi/Total
Design Concepts

# GREAT MALL OF THE BAY AREA

ARCHITECT : WAH YEE & ASSOCIATES    INTERIOR : FRCH DESIGN WORLD WIDE

Milpitas, California

1

1. Great Ships Court Entrance
2. Logo
3. Information

2

3

4. Great Planes Court Entrance
5. Great Autos Court Entrance
6. Great Planes Court

4     5

6

Filled with nostalgia and romance of journey, Great Mall of the Bay Area opened in September 1994. Its four main courts are themed after various means of travel, automobile, train, ship and plane. At the center of Great Railroad Court is a No. 49 steam locomotive which trekked its way to Milpitas during the 1890s. The waiting area is decorated with Victorian chairs used in first class, old telephone poles and memento from the old train depot.

Great Ship Court is imaged after a 1930s ocean liner deck equipped with a fountain simulating an onboard pool. Great Auto Court is designed after the garage scene from the 1950s. A '57 Ford Skyliner is displayed on a turntable with the convertible hardtop continuously retracting. Great Planes Court is decorated with the symbols from the 60's surge in the air traffic age. This 1,395,000 sq. meter giant mall was built on the old Ford assembly plant site. Traffic is conducted as a large oval track. This simple layout easily allows the customers to know where their present locations and destinations are. An information desk with a large globe with miniature trains circling around is located at the mouth of the 750 seat Great Eat food court.

7. Great Railroads Court

8. Great Ships Court

9. Great Autos Court

10. Food Court

11. Great Autos Court

12. Refreshment Stand

7

8

9

10

11

12

13. Great Ships Court
14. Directory
15. Signboard

13

14

15

## GREAT MALL OF THE BAY AREA FACT SHEET

Address : 447 Great Mall Drive, Milpitas, CA 95035

Owner : Petrie-Dierman-Kughn, VA & Ford Motor Land Development Corp.

Architect : Wah Yee & Associates, Michigan

Interior/Graphic : FRCH Design World Wide

Type : Mega Outlet Mall

Completion Date : September 1994

Total Area of Site : 607,000m²

Gross Size of Center : 1,395,000m²

Trade Area Population : 6 Million

Number of Parking Space : 6,300

Key Tenant : Saks Fifth Avenue, Marshalls, Oshman's Burlington Coat Factory, Linens'n Things, Media Play

Photos : Ken Uwabo/Total Design Concepts

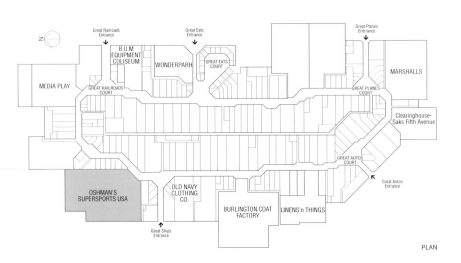

PLAN

16. Oshmans Super Sports
17. Basketball Court

16

17

## OSHMAN'S SUPER SPORTS

In 1919 Oshman's opened its first Dry Goods store in Richmond, Texas. The Super Sports is their flagship store. Concept was for shoppers to try out the desired product before purchasing. The 79,000 sq. meter store has a batting cage, basketball court, boxing ring, golf simulation, putting green, racquetball court, archery range, roller blade rink and indoor track awaiting customers.

18. Basketball Counter

19. Bicycles Counter

18

19

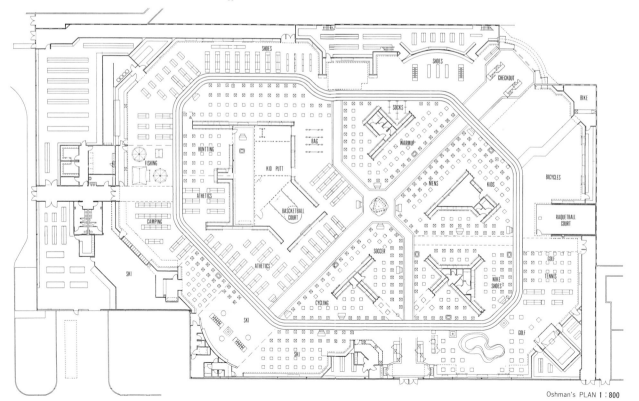

Oshman's PLAN 1 : 800

# VALENCIA TOWN CENTER

## ARCHITECT : RTKL ASSOCIATES

Valencia, California

1

2

1. Main Entrance
2. Facade at Night
3. Fountain at Rotunda
4. May Court
5. Center Court
6. Sears Court

3

4

5

7. Burried Clock at Sears Court
8. View of Center Court
9. Wall Painting
10. Food Court

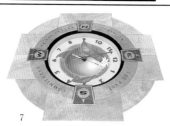

7

8

9

10

This Spanish Missionary style complex was designed to blend with the existing landscape of Santa Clarita Valley. Interior is done in Victorian style.

Anchor stores Sears, JC Penney and May, each occupy the corners of this 73,500 sq. meter total retail space. 110 retail tenants also share the 130,000 sq. meter site.

In front of the Rotunda is a walk through fountain where kid can play and inside is a carrousel. The overall design idea was derived from the English Crystal Palace. The columns and frames are painted in white. Numerous skylights and white roof panels bring the best of natural light. Around the Center Court are palm trees, vines and numerous potted plants creating arbor atrium effect. Running brook flows into a flower-like bubbling fountain. On the side of overpasses are murals depicting the old west, titled "The Orange Grove", "Our Valley", "Ranch Life" and "The People of The Valley".

11. Detail of Carousel
12. Tile Arts
13. Column and Lighting Fixture
14. Detail of Ceiling

11

12

13

14

Large scale graphics of the old orange crate labels are replicated in mosaic used at the entrance and food court. Instead of clock towers, clocks are embedded in the floor with the writings, "Pride in the Past" and "Commitment to the Future". 80% occupancy at opening, has been filled three months later.

Valencia Town Center has saved the residents of Santa Clarita from driving 20 miles to another shopping center. A plan is also in the works to convert Main Street into a promenade.

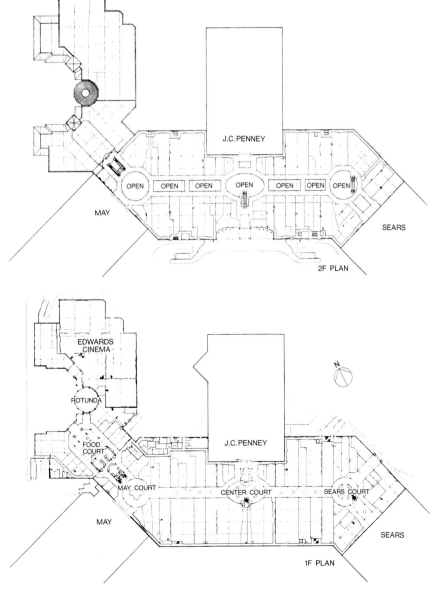

15. Signboard
16. Wall Painting
17. Signboard
18. Signboard
19. Directory

15

19

16

17

18

**VALENCIA TOWN CENTER FACT SHEET**

Address : 24140 Magic Mountain Parkway Valencia, CA 91355

Owner/Developer : Valencia Town Center Associates, The Newhall Land & Farming Co., JMB /Urban Development Co., Ltd.

Architect/Interior Design : RTKL Associates

Completion Date : October 1992

Total Area of Site : 130,000m²

Gross Size of Center : 73,500m²

Department Store Area : May(13,066m²), JC Penney(12,099m²), Sears(11,376m²)

Stores Area : 25,532m²

Food Court : 613m²

Number of Stores : 110

Number of Parking Space : 3,700

Anchor/Key Tenant : May, Sears, JC Penney

Photos : RTKL Associates

# KAAHUMANU CENTER

## ARCHITECT : ALTOON & PORTER ARCHITECTS

Kaahumanu, Hawaii

1

2

1. Main Entrance
2. Main Entrance at Night
3. View of Roof
4. 5. Super Structure
6. Center Court
7. Center Court and Food Court

3

4

5

6

7

Maui is the central resort island of Hawaii, and is visited by over 250,000 tourists a year. In 1979, the Kaahumanu Center opened in a commercial district between an airport and a governmental office area. It is on the main street of Maui. Although the site was easily accessible, the shopping center was only used by local shoppers. After several renovations, it was renewed to meet the demand of the new market. The market research showed that it could accommodate the growing population of 45,000 resides and the 110,000 customer markets.

### Design Concept

The existing anchor tenants (Sears and Liberty House) are located on both ends of the main concourse. There is a concourse between the new anchor JC Penney and other shop fronts that go across the main concourse. The basic concept of the mall is to reflect a beautiful scene of the sky of Maui. It also shows the first sailing ship that brought trade and commerce to this island which was another design motif. Images of the sailing ship are used for the roof structure of the walkway, the rest areas, and the food court. The translucent glazed roof is like a sail of an old ship with beautiful mountains and moving clouds of Maui as a backdrop. The roof is popular and appeals to the shoppers. The

8. Logo
9. Food Court
10. View of Overbridge
11. Center Court

8

9

10

11

12. Signboard
13. Lighting Fixture
14. Detail of Handrail
15. Front Facade Section
16. Site Plan

12

13

roof is well ventilated with Teflon fabric which eliminates most of the ultraviolet rays and lets in the natural light. It brings a sense of openness to the interior.

14

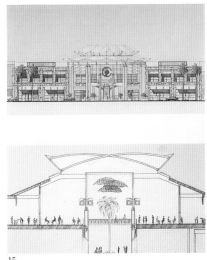

15

16

**KAAHUMANU CENTER FACT SHEET**
Address : Kaahumanu, Hawaii
Owner/Developer : Maui Land & Pineapple Co.
Architect : Altoon & Porter Architects
Type : Regional
Completion Date : 1973, Renovation/December 1994
Gross Area of Center : 55,740 m²
Anchor/Key Tenant : JC Penney, Liberty House, Sears
Photos : David Franzen, Taguchi Design

# ALOHA TOWER MARKETPLACE
## ARCHITECT : D'AGOSTINO IZZO QUIRK ARCHITECTS

Honolulu, Hawaii

1

2

3

1. Complete View
2. Facade
3. View of Aloha Tower
4. Main Entrance
5. View of Deck
6. Restaurant

4

5

6

## Project Concept and Design

The Aloha Tower Market Place opened at the end of 1994 in Oahu, Hawaii. It is remodeled after an old market place on the island. Designed upon the historical heritage of the waterfront of Honolulu, it is built near the Honolulu Tower, a focal point of the harbor. The Market Place is part of a project to reactivate the waterfront and make it more exciting, because it was fading with the end of the era of ships. The Aloha Tower Market Place has no special anchor tenants to support it and is mainly composed of 100 specialty stores, ten restaurants and a 700 seated food court. The building is a two story in a Mediterranean style with reminiscence of scenes of Honolulu in the 1930s and 40s. The location and arrangement of the shops and restaurants brings about a festival feeling of the mall, making the most this seaside location. The mall is divided into several sections. It looks small and cozy, giving visitors a warm and open feeling.

**ALOHA TOWER MARKETPLACE FACT SHEET**
Address : Honolulu, Hawaii
Developer : Aloha Tower Associates
Architect : D'Agostino Izzo Quirk Architects
Type : Festival Marketplace
Completion Date : December 1994
Gross Size of Center : 16,908 m²
Photos : David Franzen

55

7. Center Court
8. Courtyard
9. Restaurant
10. Expansion Model

7

8

9

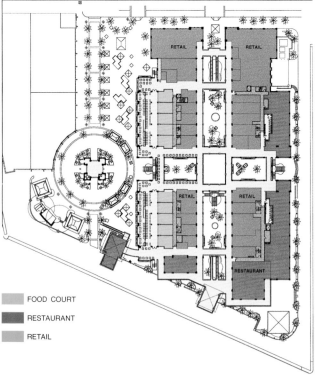

FOOD COURT

RESTAURANT

RETAIL

2F FLOOR PLAN

10

# WOODLANDS MALL

## ARCHITECT : ELBASANI & LOGAN ARCHITECTS

Woodlands, Texas

1

2

1. North Entrance
2. Main Entrance
3. Main Entrance at Evening
4. Main Entrance
5. View of Center Court

3

4

5

6. View of Center Court
7. Bird Sculpture
8. View of Mall

6

7

9. Passageway on 2nd Floor

10. Food Court

11. Food Court

12. Food Court

9

10

11

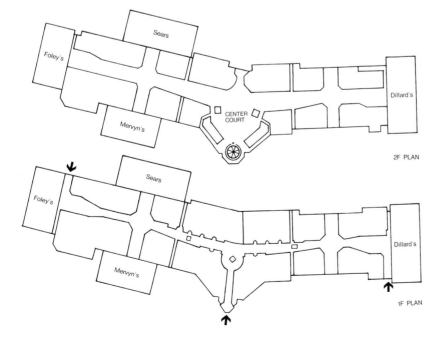

12

Woodlands Mall is a suburban mall, located 30 miles north of Houston, Texas.

The city is only 40,000 in population but has an area market of 340,000. The average income of $55,000 is the median of middle class America. At opening, it already had 95% occupancy.

Including the maple leaf shaped skylight, the complex uses 16,740 sq. meters of glass giving ample light and clean impression. Series of domes and a carrousel on the second floor gives this mall its character. Contemporary, colorful, giant metal sculptures of a bird and a fish decorate the center court. Numerous potted trees and plants give it an arbor atrium feel. The four anchor stores Dillard's, Sears, Mervyn's and Foley's are accompanied by 120 retailers and kiosks including Gap, Brookstone and the Discovery Store.

Sears

Foley's

Mervyn's

CENTER COURT

Dillard's

2F PLAN

Sears

Foley's

Mervyn's

Dillard's

1F PLAN

13. Carousel
14. 15. Lighting Fixture
16. 17. Detail of Bridge
18. Bridge and Lighting Fixture

13

Simple layout and high visibility with the convenience of 25 bridges have solved the traffic disadvantage of being second floor tenants. Having brand name stores such as Warner Brothers Studio Store, Eddy Bauer Home Collection and the Great Toy Train Shop also help to attract customers. Next door is a 10,000 seat outdoor theater, Cynthia Woods Michell Pavilion which houses the Houston Symphony during the summer. Another plan for a 17 screen, 4,200 seat movie theater will also help this complex to become an entertainment center.

18

14

15

16

17

### WOODLANDS MALL FACT SHEET

Address : 1313 Lake Woodlands Drive, The Woodlands, Texas
Owner/Developer : Homart Development Co.
Architect : Elbasani & Logan Architects, Barkeley, CA
Completion Date : October 1994
Total Area of Site : 93,000 m²
Gross Leasable Space : 32,740 m²
Number of Stores : 142
Food Court Area : 2,180 m²
Anchor / Key Tenant : Dillard's, Foley's, Mervyn's, Sears
Cost of Construction : 21 Million $
Photos : Timothy Hursley

# LAKELINE MALL
## ARCHITECT : WILLIAM GRAVES ARCHITECTS

Austin, Texas

1

2

1. Main Entrance
2. Food Court Entrance
3. View of Center Court
4. View of Center Court
5. View of Center Court

3

4

5

6. View of Mall

7. View of Mall

8. Section Sketch of Elevator Tower

9. View of Mall

10. Entertainment Sketch

6

7

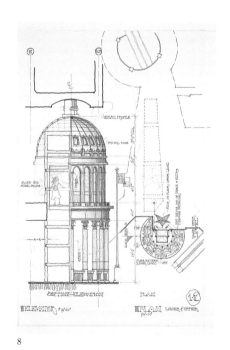

8

9

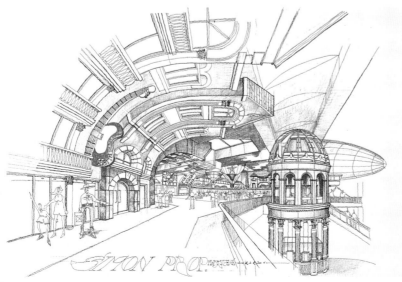

10

Austin is the capital of Texas, with more than 100,000 people employed by state and local government agencies. The most economically advantaged community in Texas, it is experiencing unprecedented growth-much of it in white-collar job and new housing valued at more than $200,000. Lakeline trade-area households have annual incomes over $50, 000. Anchors are Foley's, Dillard's, Mervyn's, Sears and JC Penney. Shoppers will also enjoy The Disney Store, Gap, Structure, Express, Victoria Secret, Beall's and approximately 120 Speciality stores, nearly 30 are coming to Austin for the first time.

Imagine Austin reinvented by Disney or Dali. Landmark buildings bend under a blue and white neon-lit sky; the clock from the University of Texas dangles overhead, and nondescript face of man with a neat gray mustache and aviator sunglasses extends gargoyle-like from one of the warped building facades. An elevator is surrounded by a canary yellow version the state Capital dome, which competes with a Goodyear Blimp.

11. Food Court
12. Ceiling Plan
13. Food Court

11

12

13

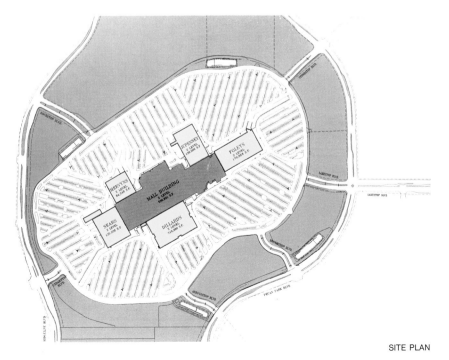

SITE PLAN

The Center Court, a whimsical, light-hearted city facaded environment captures the mall patrons in a metamorphic warp where reality is bent to the limit (city ordinance limits no building can be taller than the city hall). Hot air balloons float above the city, billboards and blade signs all purposefully aimed at entertainment, fun and "getting together".

14. Signboard Sketch
15. 3D-Clock Sketch
16. Mall Sketch

LAKELINE MALL SIGNAGE STUDIES . DETAIL          BY McBRIDE CO.

14

Side view

Front View

15

16

## LAKELINE MALL FACT SHEET

Address : 13492 Research Blvd., Austin, Texas 78750

Developer/Owner : Simon Property Group

Architect/Interior Design : William Graves Architects

Entertainment Area Design : The McBride Company

Completion date : August 1995

Total Area of Site : 105,000m²

Gross Leasable Area : 86,225m²

Food Court Area : 605 m²

Number of Stores : 125

Anchor/Key Tenant : Sears, Mervyn's, JC Penney, Foley's, Dillard's

Number of Parking Space : 4,650

Photos : William Graves Architects

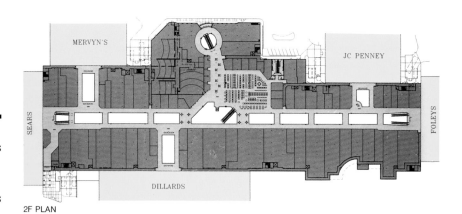

2F PLAN

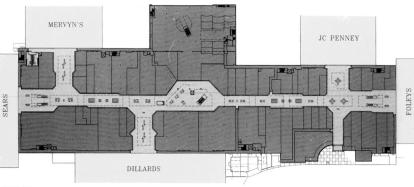

1F PLAN

# CHICAGO PLACE
## ARCHITECT : SKIDMORE, OWINGS & MERRILL

Chicago, Illinois

1

2

3

1. Facade
2. Entrance
3. Glass Facade and Symbolmark
4. North Michigan Avenue
5. Entrance

## North Michigan Avenue

North Michigan Avenue is a shopping mecca. It is called the " magnificent mile " or the " one wonderful mile ".

There are many well-known American and European stores like Neiman-Marcus, Saks Fifth Avenue, Bloomingdale's, Chanel, Gucci, Tiffany's, Cartier, Crate & Barrel, Nike, Banana Republic, The Gap and many others. Water Tower Place was opened in 1975 and it now attracts 25 million people a year. One of the best selling shopping centers per square foot is this mall. It accumulated 600 dollars per square foot in 1990. A complex called 900 North Michigan and a classy Four Season's Hotel and condo opened in the fall of 1989. Chicago Place with its 272 condominiums opened in the fall of 1990. The center has dynamic atriums surrounded by anchor tenants and specialty shops. Visitors have easy access from Michigan Avenue to the mall lobby.

This shows an intriguing model of a high rise shopping mall plan.

## Chicago Place

With a row of beautiful trees on Michigan Avenue, Chicago Place is reminiscent of an old Chicago shopping street. It reflects images of facades occupied by Carson Pirie Scott & Co., by Louis Sullivan, Marshall Field by Daniel Burnham. The interior

4

5

6. Saks Fifth Avenue Entrance
7. Street Lamp
8. View of Atrium

6

7

8

and exterior of Chicago Place was designed using typical Chicago architecture. It is a very acceptable and familiar style for the local people. Its human scale and comfortable shopping environment are noteworthy. The Chicago-based architect, Skidmore, Owings and Merrill designed this project. Sussman Prejza worked on the graphics and the signs. The developer is Brookfield Development. Chicago Place is composed of an eight floor shopping center and a forty three floor level set-back condo with 272 rooms which was designed by another architect.

The entrance is two and a half floor levels high(12 meters). An atrium of eight floor levels is in the center of the building. A focal point of the atrium is designed for the visitors for easy orientation of the stores. The interior is arranged around the atrium to the eighth floor. Entering form North Michigan Avenue, the visitor will see Saks Fifth Avenue, an anchor tenant, on the right side. It is occupied from the first to the seventh floors. Fifty shops and ten restaurants, including fast food eateries, restaurant cafes, and others occupy the top floor. Each floor has ten shops around a stairwell and creates a cozy walk space.

On the top floor garden, there is an oblong arch-shaped roof which runs toward the street.

9. Lobby
10. Sculpture
11. Stores at Atrium
12. Handrail
13. Lobby

9

10

11

12

13

14. Room & Board
15. Chiasso

14

15

The light dramatically comes through the skylight and emphasizes the vertical lines of the atrium. A nice landscape of a garden with plants and a fountain surround a restaurant, a cafe, and a fast food restaurant. It reminds the visitor of the 19th or early 20th century glass house or winter gardens of Europe.

People feel comfortable to see a winding stream running through overgrown plants. It is a kind of an oasis in a big city, far from the noise and the crowded busy streets. From the garden the visitor sees the whole view of North Michigan Avenue, Lake Michigan, the historical Water Tower, and other landmark architectural structures in Chicago.

**CHICAGO PLACE FACT SHEET**

Address : 700 North Michigan Avenue, Chicago, Illinois
Developer : Brookfield Development Inc.
Architect : Shopping Center / Skidmore, Owings & Merrill
Type : Regional
Completion Date : September 1990
Gross Size of Center : 29,728m²
Trade Area Population : 8 Million
Anchor/Key Tenant : Saks Fifth Avenue, Room & Board
Photos : S.O.M., Sussman/Prejza, Taguchi Design

FACADE RENDERING

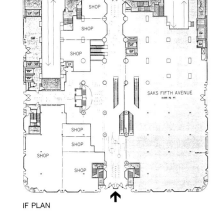

IF PLAN

77

# 900 NORTH MICHIGAN

## ARCHITECT : PERKINS & WILL, KOHN PEDERSEN FOX ASSOCIATES

Chicago, Illinois

16

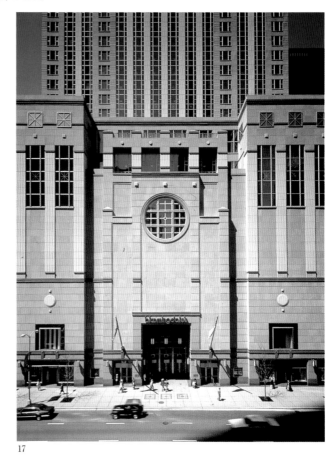

17

18

19

16. Facade
17. Entrance
18. Circle Window
19. Handrail
20. View of Atrium
21. Stores at Atrium

20

21

## 900 North Michigan

This sixty six floor level complex of offices, condos, high class hotels, and shopping centers is located four blocks north of Chicago Place. The total construction cost was $450 million and the total floor area is 250, 830 square meters. The eighth floor level shopping center faces North Michigan Avenue and keeps in harmony with the traditional style surroundings of Chicago Place.

Cream white and a pale green limestone cover the building and granite, lime, and marble are used for the facade to give a friendly impression to people who pass by.

### 900 NORTH MICHIGAN FACT SHEET

Address : 900 North Michigan Avenue, Chicago, Illinois

Developer : JMB/Urban Development Co., Chicago

Architect : Perkins & Will, Kohn Pedersen Fox Associates

Type : Regional

Completion Date : Autumn 1988/Retail, Bloomingdale's Spring 1989/Four Seasons Hotel Autumn 1990/Henri Bendel

Gross Size of Center : 41,805m²

Number of Parking Space : 1,450

Trade Area Population : 8 Million

Anchor/Key Tenant : Bloomingdale's, Henri Bendel

Photos : Kohn Pedersen Fox Associates

22. Interior Rendering
23. Entrance Lobby
24. Bridge and Floor Pattern
25. Storefront Drawing

22

23

24

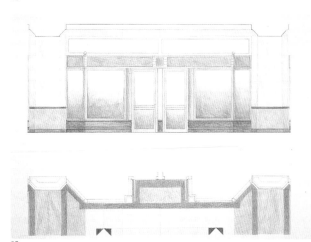

25

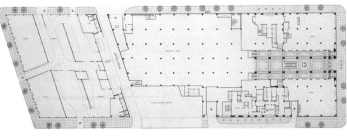

IF PLAN

# NAVY PIER

## ARCHITECT : VOA ASSOCIATES, BENJAMIN THOMPSON ASSOCIATES

Chicago, Illinois

1

1. Entrance Gate
2. Logo
3. Complete View
4. Main Entrance
5. Fountain
6. Looking at Main Entrance from Center of Pier

2

3

4

5

6

Navy Pier was the first of five piers planned to be built near the mouth of Chicago River emptying into Lake Michigan in 1916. After completing one at a cost of $4.5 million, the project was halted. With the outbreak of WW I in 1917, the pier was turned over to the Navy. Peace time and decrease in shipping eventually closed the pier all together. Major renovation was completed in May 1995 for $190 million. The overall length was extended to 960 meters. The total site of 200,000 sq. meters is roughly divided into three parts : Family Pavilion/Crystal Garden, The Park and Festival Hall.

Near the entrance to the pier is the Family Pavilion/Crystal Garden which houses the Chicago Children's Museum, I-MAX Theater, retail shops and restaurants. I-MAX Theater projects 3D images onto a 60' x 80' screen with 20,000W audio output. Crystal Garden is a 6 story glass structure with an indoor fountain and filled with tropical plantations and flowers. The Park has a 15 story high Ferris wheel, a carrousel, a pool during summer and an ice skate rink in winter. Skyline Theater is a 1, 500 seat outdoor facility.

7. Illinois Market Place
8. Passageway at Park
9. View of Crystal Garden
10. Ferris Wheel

7

8

9

Festival Hall houses a 16,000 sq. meter exhibition hall and a 4,460 sq. meter conference hall. The beer garden atop the two halls is a favorite resting spot.

The south side of the pier retains the original purpose of harboring cruises and charter boats. Annually over 4 million people visit Navy Pier.

10

11. Inside View of Crystal Garden
12. Inside View of Family Pavilion
13. Crystal Garden (Under Construction)

11

12

13

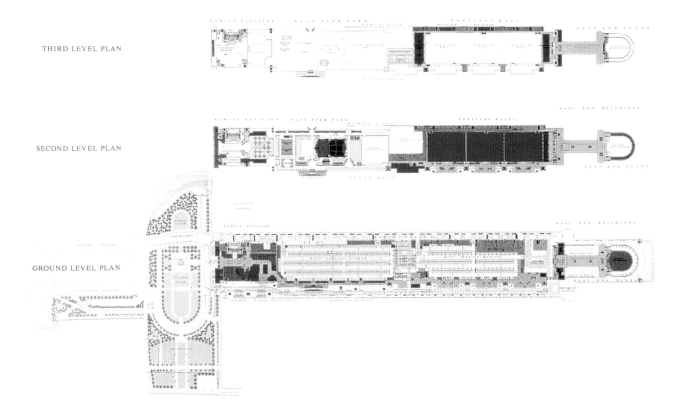

THIRD LEVEL PLAN

SECOND LEVEL PLAN

GROUND LEVEL PLAN

14. Inside View of Family Pavilion

15. Performance & Kids

16. Cart

17. Cart

18. Flag

19. Signboard

14

15

16

17

18

19

**NAVY PIER FACT SHEET**

Address : 600E Grand Ave., Chicago, IL 60611

Developer/Owner : Metropolitan Pier & Exposition Authority

Architect : VOA Associates, Benjamin Thompson Associates

Completion Date : July 1995

Total Area of Site : 202,300m²

Food Court Area : 2,325m²

Chicago Children Museum Area : 4,650m²

Crystal Garden Area : 3,000m²

Festival Hall Area : 20,270m²

Number of I-MAX : 440 Sheets

Number of Parking Space : 1,150

Cost of Construction : 2 Million $

Photos : Ken Uwabo/Total Design Concepts, VOA

# THE SOMERSET COLLECTION
## ARCHITECT : JPRA ARCHITECTS

Troy, Michigan

1

2

3

4

1. Rotunda Facade
2. Before
3. Entrance (Before)
4. Main Entrance

5

6

7

8

9

10

The new Somerset Collection in Detroit, Michigan was renovated from an old single story shopping center that was opened in 1969. The eighteen month renovation took place, but all the shops were kept open. Tenants and merchandise were chosen from upper class and high fashion stores for the new Somerset Collection. Detroit has a population of 2,500,000 in the metropolitan area, making it the largest city in Michigan. But Detroit is missing the high class and upscale shopping centers that other cities have.

Therefore, the Somerset Collection was built in the fall of 1992 as the most prestigious mall in the area. It has been inviting a crowd of many shoppers since then.

**Project Concept and Design**

The Somerset Collection is located next to a highway where cars speed by at an average of 60 miles per hour. Therefore, the mall needed an attractive character and outlook to catch the driver's attention as they pass by. To visually attract people's attention, the height of the building was risen from 11.1 meters to 12.6 meters. For those who approached the mall from the highway, a row of trees and plants lie in a street line to greet them. The formal atmosphere and soft texture of the building impress the shoppers. There is a three floor

91

11. View of Rotunda
12. View of Center Court
13. View of Center Court
14. View of Center Court

11

12

parking lot that is connected to the shopping center by a bridge on the second floor. The shopping center has a simple layout with the anchor tenants at both ends. An oval roof rotunda was built eighteen meters from the building. It was placed to display elegance around the front of the building.

The exterior design of the mall reflects the style of the Cranbrook Art School by Eero Saarinen. The pale brown stone and dark brick texture create a sophisticated atmosphere. The full height of the glazed windows and rotundas allow visitors who pass by the mall to view the activities of the insides of the mall. There are entrances on both sides of the rotunda and the approach area looks more like a gorgeous theater lobby to a concert hall than an entrance to a mall.

13

14

15. View of Mall
16. View of Mall
17. View of Mall
18. Site Plan
19. Somerset Collection North 1st Floor Plan

15

16

17

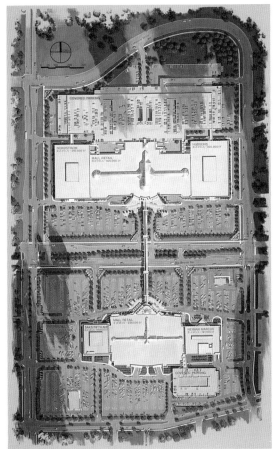

18

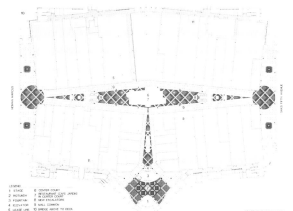

19

## THE SOMERSET COLLECTION FACT SHEET

Address : Troy, Michigan

Owner/Developer : Frankel/Forbes-Cohen Associates

Architect : JPRA Architects

Type : Regional

Completion Date : 1969 Renovation/Expansion /September 1992 Somerset Collection North/ August 1996

Gross Size of Center : 46,450m²

Anchor/Key Tenant : Neiman Marcus, Saks Fifth Avenue

Photos : Balthazar Korab, Laszio Regos

20. Somerset Collection North Rendering
21. Grand Court Rendering
22. Facade and Skyway by CG

The rotunda has fountain and semi-circular stairs that lead to the second floor. The floor of the rotunda is a beautiful geometric pattern in marble with palm trees along the glazed walls. Therefore, there is still a warm kind of feeling in the atmosphere from the palm trees even in the harsh winters of Michigan. There are always various activities, events, and fashion shows. The seethrough elevator at the rotunda, dramatically takes customers up to the second floor.

20

21

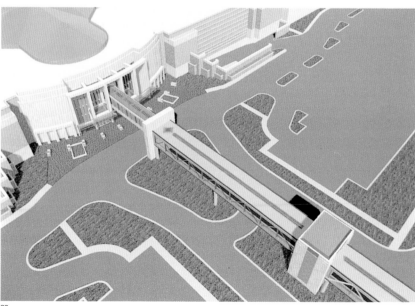

22

# TOWER CITY CENTER

## ARCHITECT : RTKL ASSOCIATES

Cleveland, Ohio

1

1. View of Station Court
2. Facade of South Side
3. Steam Concourse Entrance
4. Skylight Concourse Entrance
5. View of Station Court
6. Passageway at 3rd Floor

2

3

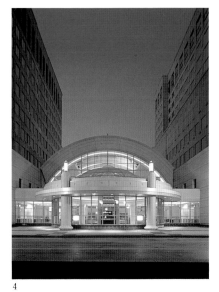

4

5

6

7. Metro Entrance
8. View of Skylight Concourse
9. Steam Diner Food Court Entrance
10. 11. Steam Diner Food Court
12. Lighting Fixture

Tower City Center is one of the most ambitious urban development effort ever undertaken in the United States. The waterfront mixed-use center is structured around the redevelopment of Cleveland's historic Terminal Tower complex, with the retail portion located within historic Union Station and above an existing transit stop that serves 120,000 passengers daily. In the early 1980's, a retail-driven mixed-use Tower City Center was planned.

The ten year effort would ultimately cost $450 million. Currently complete are The Avenue, a 380,000 sq. ft. three level retail mall with 12-plex cinema and 1,200 seats Steam Diner food court; The new 300,000 sq. ft. Skylight Office Tower; and the new 209 room Ritz Carlton Hotel. The new complex was architecturally worked within the established site and existing buildings, as well as within the historic storefronts and other architectural elements. Inside the Station Court, the once cramped and confused series of escalator entrances and ticket booths have been consolidated into a single grand space. For The Avenue the design challenge was to make an old railroad station into a retail center while still evoking the feeling of the historic station. The Steam Diner food court is a lively accent on The Avenue.

7

8

9

10

11

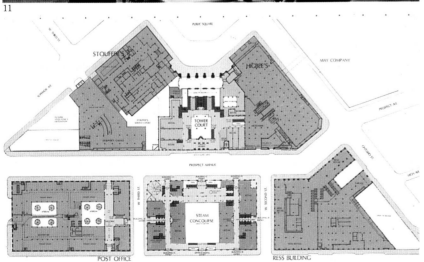

POST OFFICE  RESS BUILDING

1F PLAN

## TOWER CITY CENTER FACT SHEET

Address : Public Square, Downtown Cleveland, Ohio

Owner/Developer : Tower City Development

Architect : RTKL Associates Inc., Dallas, Texas

Completion Date : November 1991

Total Area of Site : 50,600m² (Phase1)

Number of Parking Space : 3,600

Steam Diner Food Court Area : 1,100m²(1, 200Sheets)

12

⟨THE AVENUE⟩

Total Area of Site : 10,000m²

Gross Leasable Area : 32,600m²

Stores : 150

Cost of Construction : 90 Million $

Anchor/Key Tenant : Brooks Brothers, Bally of Switzerland, Disney, Liz Claiborne, The Limited

⟨THE OFFICE TOWER⟩

Total Area of Site : 4,046m²

Cost of Construction : 66 Million $

⟨POST OFFICE⟩

Total Area of Site : 4,046m²

Cost of Construction : 44 Million $

Photos : Scott McDonald, David Whitecomb

# CLEVELAND ARCADE
## ARCHITECT : KAPLAN, McLAUGHLIN, DIAZ

Cleveland, Ohio

1

1. View of Mall
2. View of Mall
3. Bird's-Eye View of Mall

2

3

Nicknamed "Cleveland's Crystal Palace", this arcade was initially built to connect two downtown office towers. At the time of opening, it was the largest arcade with 112 shops. It used the highest technology of the time to support its glass ceiling.

In 1978, KMD revitalized the old arcade. The Roman Byzantine structure was re-enforced. Brass railings and metalwork have been restored. All 1,800 window glass were replaced. The reborn Cleveland Arcade became a National Historical Landmark.

4. Ornament

4

**CLEVELAND ARCADE FACT SHEET**
Address : 210 The Arcade, Cleveland, Ohio 44114
Owner : The Arcade Ltd.
Developer : Conner, McLaughlin/Oppman
Architect : Kaplan, McLaughlin, Diaz
Total Area of Site : 7,900m²
Gross Leasable Area : 27,900m²
Number of Stores : 121
Photos : Thom Abel

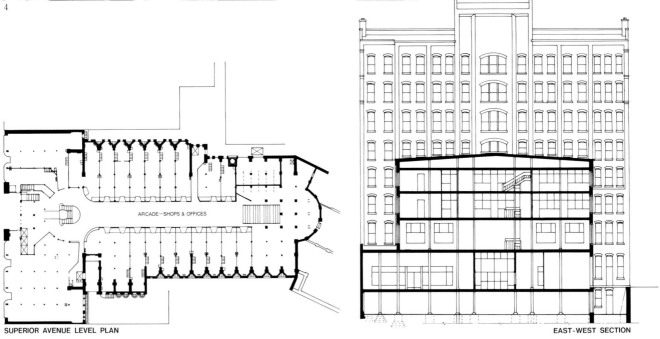

SUPERIOR AVENUE LEVEL PLAN

ARCADE—SHOPS & OFFICES

EAST-WEST SECTION

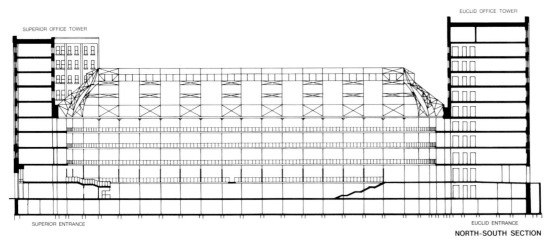

SUPERIOR OFFICE TOWER

EUCLID OFFICE TOWER

SUPERIOR ENTRANCE

EUCLID ENTRANCE

NORTH-SOUTH SECTION

# SAINT LOUIS GALLERIA
## ARCHITECT : HELLMUTH, OBATA & KASSABAUM

Saint Louis, Missouri

1

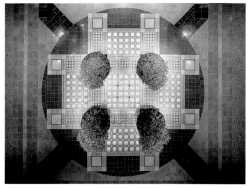

2

1. Main Entrance at Night
2. Floor Design
3. View of Garden Court
4. View of Mall
5. View of Garden Court

## Location

The Saint Louis Galleria is located near the intersections of two highways.

It is accessible by a ten minute drive to the west from downtown St. Louis. There are about twelve hundred companies occupied in a sixteen hundred meter radius around the area. Eighteen thousand people work and 80,000 visit this area everyday. Plaza Frontenac is located in Frontenac, which was ranked as one of the twenty best upper class residential districts in the United States. Plaza Frontenac is situated about eight kilometers away from the St. Louis Galleria. The metropolitan area of St. Louis has over 24 million residents. The St. Louis Galleria and Plaza Frontenac target a market of 1,100,000 customers from this population. The average annual income of the customers is $112,000 in 1992. St. Louis Galleria was opened in 1986 as a super regional mall. It was renovated and extended in 1991. Plaza Frontenac was opened in 1974 and renovated in 1994.

3

4

5

6. View of Atrium
7. View of Mall
8. Storefront of Brooks Brothers

## Saint Louis Galleria

One of most important conditions that the super regional mall requires is that the mall should be easily accessed and recognized by every driver on the highway. The St. Louis Galleria meets this requirement. The St. Louis Galleria opened in 1986 with only one anchor tenant, Dillard's.

Renovation and extension was performed so that the Galleria would be available for the growing population and market in 1991. The two story St. Louis Galleria was designed using an English garden-style architecture as a model. The focal point of the mall is a garden court with an atrium. The center of the garden court is Marble Plaza which was designed a couple steps lower than the main floor to accommodate a pond and a fountain made of marble. The light shining from the skylight reflects off the pond and makes the area brighter. Concerts and fashion shows can also be held on a stage that can be created by simply draining the water from the pond.

There are flower beds and cafes all around the pond. A French style cafe located on the second floor has a good view of the pond. Every plant and sculpture in the mall is beautifully lit up at night.

6

7

8

9. View of Mall
10. Wall Art
11. Directory
12. Entrance Signboard

9

12

10

11

FAMOUS-BAR

GARDEN COURT

LORD & TAYLOR

DILLARD'S

1F PLAN

**SAINT LOUIS GALLERIA FACT SHEET**
Address : Clayton & Brentwood Blvd., Saint
Louis, Missouri
Developer : Hycel Properties Co.
Architect : Hellmuth, Obata & Kassabaum
Type : Super Regional
Completion Date : 1986, Expansion/1991
Gross Size of Center : 109,622m²
Trade Area Population : 1.1 Million
Anchor/Key Tenant : Dillard's, Famous-Bar,
Lord & Taylor
Photos : Alise O'Brien

# PLAZA FRONTENAC

## ARCHITECT : HELLMUTH, OBATA & KASSABAUM

Saint Louis, Missouri

1

2

3

4

1. View of Center Court
2. View of Neiman Marcus Court
3. View of Rest Area
4. Rest Area at 2nd Floor
5. Rest Area at 1st Floor

5

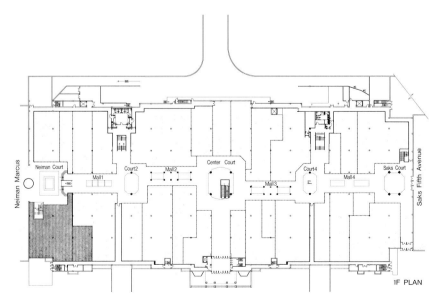

1F PLAN

Plaza Frontenac opened in 1974 in a quiet and up-scale residential area. It was renovated in 1994. The Plaza targets high income customers. The shopping center is not big and occupies 45,866 square meters, with Neiman Marcus and Saks Fifth Avenue as anchor tenants. The two big tenants are situated on either ends of the largest concourse. The mall was planned in a simple layout. The renovation was designed on a country club atmosphere where the customers can shop and dine comfortable. The design of the addition would still be kept classy. At first the old wooden floor was planned to replaced by a marble one. But in accordance with opposition from the locals who wanted to keep the same images of the old shopping center, the old floor was restored and polished. An important trend in shopping centers is developing where it has become vital to create an at-home atmosphere as well as special public rest areas more like a hotel lounge, for the shoppers.

## PLAZA FRONTENAC FACT SHEET

Address : 1701S Lindbergh Blvd., Frontenac, Missouri
Developer : Capital Land Co.
Architect : Hellmuth, Obata & Kassabaum
Type : Regional
Completion Date : 1974, Renovation/1994
Gross Size of Center : 40,886m²
Trade Area Population : 1.1 Million
Anchor/Key Tenant : Neiman Marcus, Saks Fifth Avenue

6. View of Lounge
7. Concierge Desk
8. Floor Pattern

6

7

8

# ROOSEVELT FIELD
## ARCHITECT : RTKL ASSOCIATES

New York

1

2

3

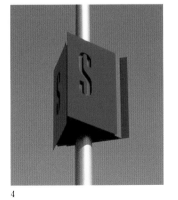

4

5

1. Main Entrance
2. Sub Entrance
3. Signboard
4. 5. Parking Lot Signboard

6

6. View of Mall
7. View of Mall
8. View of Mall

7

8

Roosevelt Field, in Long Island, New York, is one of the oldest shopping malls in the east coast. It was first opened in 1956. The first American indoor shopping center in Minneapolis, Minnesota was completed that same year. The original building were of a strip-outdoor type with fifty shops.

It was designed by I.M. Pei in 1968, it was renovated as an indoor mall and was also extended in 1974 to have the largest shopping center in the east coast. Its annual sale is top ranking at $450 million. In 1993, a $150 million renovation and extension project tied up complicated traffic flows and transformed the boxy stereotypical buildings into a more modern form in order to invite more local customers.

9. Winding Stairs
10. View of Dome
11. Elevator Shaft
12. Detail of Kiosk
13. Stairs

9

10

11

12

13

14

15

16

17

## Location

Roosevelt Field is in Garden City next to New York City and is easily accessible from the highway which runs from south to north on Long Island.

The site used to be Roosevelt Field Airport where Lindberg, Hearst, Earhart, and other famous aviators took off. Later the airport became a commercial district and office buildings, universities, and coliseums developed.

## Project Concept and Design

This shopping mall has a capacity to hold four department stores. It is fifth largest mall in the United States. In consideration of the regulations about the limitations of extension, the building had to be two stories for a new food court. Tenant space covering 14,864 square meters for sixty shops was also added with the second floor. It would allow access to each department store by the second floor. A common way to renew a boxy shopping mall is to use many skylights, domes, arches, homey rest areas, and taking advantage of the environmental graphic design. Roosevelt Field is where one sees a pale colored dome with skylights and public rest areas at busy sections of the mall. It makes the interior look brighter and more spacious.

18. Logo of Zeppelin
19. Food Court
20. Food Court

18

19

20

21. Food Court
22. Top of Airship
23. Storefront of Food Court
24. Column Detail

21

22

23

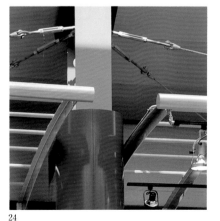

24

The new food court is the focal point, situated on the second floor. It has fourteen tenants and 1,000 seats. The food court in an oval plan is surrounded by walkways that run parallel to it. The theme of the food court is a Zeppelin. The bottom of the gigantic airship is designed to float above the store front.

**ROOSEVELT FIELD FACT SHEET**
Address : Garden City, New York
Developer : Corporate Property Investors
Architect : RTKL Associates/Dallas
Food Court/Sign : Sussman/Prejza
Type : Super Regional
Completion Date : 1956
Renovation/Expansion Date : 1968, 1974, 1993
Gross Size of Center : 185,800m²
Number of Parking Space : 9,000
Anchor/Key Tenant : Macy's, A&S, JC Penney, Sterns
Photos : RTKL Associates/Dallas, Sussman/Prejza, Taguchi Design

25

26

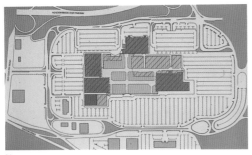

29

27

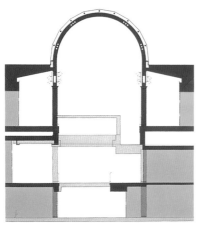

30

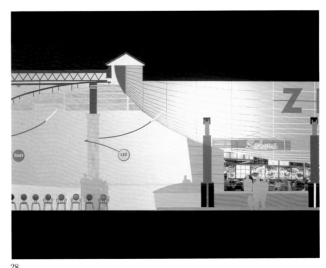

28

# THE SHOPS AT PRUDENTIAL CENTER
## ARCHITECT : SIKES JENNINGS KELLY & BREWER

Boston, Massachusetts

1

2

1. Arcade Entrance
2. Arcade Entrance at Night
3. Outside Public Area

## Location

The Boston metropolitan area holds 3 million people and most of them are people who earn high incomes. With a museum, a concert hall, a theater, a library, and other cultural centers, the Prudential Center area is considered the most fabulous part of the city. Gradual depopulation in the central part of the city is regarded as a problem. However, the big cities in the north leave their downtown areas quite active. This area is attractive because it can provide a comfortable and convenient environment, particularly for people who live during the long and cold winter. The Prudential Center has a high rise apartment and 27,000 high income residents in an 800 meter radius.

Forty two thousand people work near the center. The Hynes Convention Center, near the Prudential Center, was doubled in size and several thousand people visit there everyday. Totally, over 500,000 shoppers visit there each year.

However even under these circumstances, the center was not very successful even though it had Saks Fifth Avenue and Lord & Taylor as anchor tenants before the renovation.

3

4

4. View of Mall

5. View of Center Court

6. View of Bridge Court

7. View of Mall

5

6

7

8. Storefront
9. View of Fashion Court
10. Storefront

## Project Concept

With support from the local community, renovation projects of the center started in the middle 1980s. The mayor of Boston chose several citizens to set up a committee for them to discuss about the redevelopment of the area.

The following five requirements were decided for the master plan. First, peripheral facilities were to be united with the center. Second, traffic flows for pedestrians would be simplified. Third an arcade would be designed to fit the landscape. The cost of the extension of the adjacent highway must also be minimized. Finally, each phase of the master plan was to be executed independently.

The master plan called for two new office buildings, three condominiums, and newly renovated and extended commercial facilities. The plan was divided into five stages. The construction period would take from about seven to ten years.

The important element of the plan concept was how to match the new project to the existing surroundings. Corridors linking each facility were designed as arcaded streets. Commercial facilities were designed upon models of European ones like the Burlington Arcade in London.

8

9

10

11. Arcade Signboard and Ceiling
12. Planter
13. Signboard

11

12

13

The nine meter wide arcade has shops on both sides of it and connects the department stores, office buildings, and the outsides of the facility. Each cross section has a court.

The largest court is used for certain events and gatherings. There is a Fashion Court in front of Saks Fifth Avenue, a Hynes Court in front of the Convention Center, and a Bridge Court in front of Copley Plaza. The arcade has a traditional gothic style panels and columns. The contrast of geometric hard steel parts and the soft colors make a nice combination. The sunshine comes through the arch ceiling and it casts a beautiful shade of the city scape onto the floor.

**THE SHOPS AT PRUDENTIAL CENTER FACT SHEET**

Address : 800 Boylston Street, Boston, Massachusetts

Developer : The Prudential Realty Group

Retail Management : Hahn Property Management Corp.

Type : Regional

Completion Date : October 1993

Gross Size of Center : 19,700m²

Number of Parking Space : 3,900

Trade Area Population : 2.8 Million

Anchor/Key Tenant : Saks Fifth Avenue, Lord & Tayler

Photos : Prudential Center

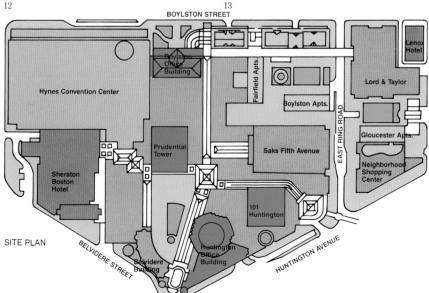

SITE PLAN

# CAMBRIDGESIDE GALLERIA

## ARCHITECT : ARROWSTREET

Cambridge, Massachusetts

1

2

1. Facade at Night
2. Facade
3. South Facade at Night
4. View of Atrium

3

4

The first floor of the Cambridgeside Galleria was designed for shops and restaurants to be a part of a festive atmosphere. The second and third floors would be available for the high-end fashionable tenants. The Galleria, like the shops at the Prudential Center, were well arranged and planned as a shopping center. They both put under consideration of the pedestrians, the town scape, and the neighborhood, and were able to put them together effectively. On the north side, there is a Canal Park where the Charles River leads to a small bay. The concourse of the Galleria starts from the fountain of the park to another park in the south part of the same project. The site of this project used to be a demolished old warehouse, but was cleverly transformed using much steel and glass. Shops are located around the central atrium. A food court is located along the bay.

**CAMBRIDGESIDE GALLERIA FACT SHEET**
Address : 100 Cambridgeside Place, Cambridge, Massachusetts
Developer : New England Development
Architect : Arrowstreet Inc.
Type : Super Regional
Completion Date : September 1990
Gross Size of Center : 74,320m²
Number of Parking Space : 2,000
Trade Area Population : 2.8 Million
Anchor/Key Tenant : Filene's, Lechmere, Sears
Photos : Taguchi Design

5. Passageway on 3rd Floor
6. Looking up Glass Ceiling
7. Food Court

5

6

7

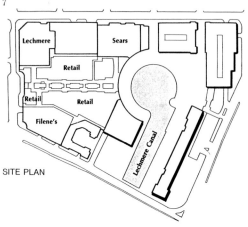

SITE PLAN

128

# NATICK MALL

## ARCHITECT : ARROWSTREET

Natick, Massachusetts

1

1. View of Mall
2. Main Entrance
3. Main Entrance (Before)
4. View of Mall (Before)
5. View of Mall (Under Costruction)
6. View of Mall

## Location

The population of Boston is the seventh largest in the United States. The east side of the city faces the sea and expressways which connects to New York.

Natick is a suburb thirty kilometers west of Boston, and is located three kilometers south from the highways. It is a typical suburban town with rich greens. Natick Mall was an early type of Indoor shopping centers. It was built in the 1960s and renovated in October 1994 with new technology to meet the new market's needs of this age. The renewed mall is double the size, it was transformed into the first super regional mall in this area.

## Project Concept and Design

Over seventy percent of the local customers are female, therefore the mall was planned to appeal towards women. It can be said that this is the first mall that specifically targets female customers. Generally, the women buy and shop more than the men. The malls have to be designed to meet the women's needs. The design concept of Natick Mall is to create a soft and entertaining shopping environment.

2

3

4

5

6

7. View of Mall
8. Public Area
9. Elevator
10. Detail of Elevator
11. View of Ceiling
12. Floor Pattern

7

8

9

10

11

12

The original single story building was demolished and a new two story was rebuilt at the same site. The basic style of the new building is a Victorian style that is a popular style amongst women. It was designed upon a New England style and is romantic, conservative shape with beautiful hand-made iron fences and decorations on the gates. The mall is arranged in a typical floor plan. The shops align both sides of a concourse, and anchor tenants are on both ends of it. The interior uses a lot of curves, emphasizing the New England landscape. The decorations on the ceilings, the patterns on the walkways, and the ornamental details create a cheerful atmosphere. It has a feeling of an conservatory with the ceiling and skylights in a S-curve which also accentuates the long promenade. The curved ceiling is lit up softly and the skylights let the natural light show through. The ceiling is reminiscent of an English conservatory with spoke-like pipes that support the ceiling and connect columns. The Victorian style is reflected through the handrails on the second floor, and the glazed cage-like elevators, that are the focal point.

The flower patterns on the floor, the elevators, and architectural ornaments remind the visitor of a conservatory with a gentle backdrop.

13. Food Court
14. Food Court
15. Storefront
16. Facade Rendering

13

14

15

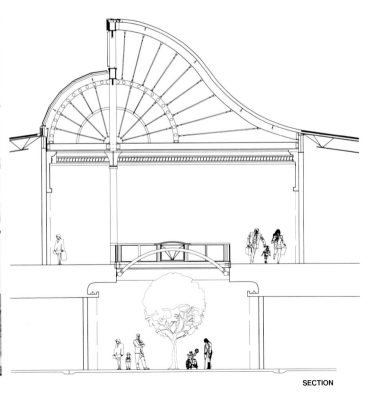

SECTION

134

16

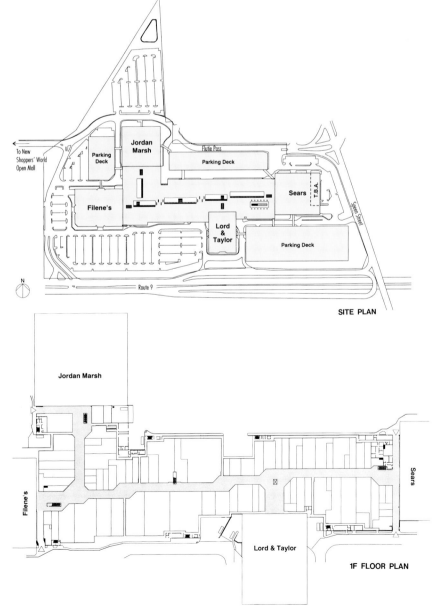

SITE PLAN

1F FLOOR PLAN

**NATICK MALL FACT SHEET**

Address : Natick, Massachusetts

Owner/Developer : Homart

Architect : Arrowstreet Inc.

Type : Super Regional

Renovation Date : October 1994

Anchor/Key Tenant : Filene's, Jordan Marsh, Lord & Taylor, Sears

Photos : Robert E. Mikrut

17. 18. Floor Pattern
19. Plant Pattern
20. Lighting Fixture and Moulding
21. Handrail
22. Handrail
23. Signboard

17

18

19

20

21

22

23

# PHIPPS PLAZA

## ARCHITECT : THOMPSON, VENTULLET, STAINBACK & ASSOCIATES

Atlanta, Georgia

1

2

3

1. Facade
2. Entrance
3. Entrance Landscape
4. View of Center Court
5. View of Concource
6. Concource

4

5

6

## location

Atlanta, a big city representing the southern states of America, held the Olympics in 1996. It made drastic progress and attracted many big companies, because the city has a nice business environment compared to other cities in the Untied States. Office buildings and classy hotels are built in the French beaux-arts style in the gorgeous residential areas. It creates a business center in the suburbs. Phipps Plaza along with Saks Fifth Avenue and Lord & Taylor as anchor tenants, opened in 1969 ant it targeted high-end customers. Now it extends its market, allowing easy access by highway. In the close vicinity of Phipps Plaza, there is also Lenox Square which is the largest mall in the south. A Four Season's Hotel is also located nearby.

## Project Design and Concept

In 1986 when a new owner acquired Phipps Plaza, it did not attract as many customers as the adjacent Lenox Plaza was getting. It was time to renovate because the tenants' images looked outdated. A plan of building as access loop on the nearby highway was submitted. The highway was eventually connected with Phipps Plaza after negotiations with the local government.

7. Lobby
8. Center Court
9. Handrail
10. Center Court

Needless to say, it worked very well. This market extension, or critical mass, urged the renovation and soon a new department called Parisian was annexed.

This new mall is elegantly designed for both low and high income bracket customers and also has a comfortable and at-home feeling. The architectural design was commissioned to Thompson, Ventullet, Stainback & Associates, Inc. The design concept is a combination of images of the old south and those of the new Atlanta. Classical details and a proportion of early southern style architecture like those of a mansion in a plantation are used for the interior.

center court, he feels an atmosphere of a gaudy mansion in the south with two grand and gentle sloping staircases with elegant handrails. There are also beautifully decorated columns, moldings and decorations on the ceiling walls, a beautifully patterned marble floor, and a chandelier above. The concourses in the mall have several public space areas which are to be used by the visitor as an rest area. It is characterized with columns, floor patterns, skylights, walls with decorations and this all makes up the whole concept of the mall. Therefore, the mall is not too overwhelming but more on a human scale. A lounge with leather sofas and a coffee table

7

8

9

11. Food Court
12. Food Court
13. Column Detail
14. Sky Light
15. Floor at Anchor Tenants

creates a comfortable environment for the visitor.

Classical proportions, geometric
patterns on the ceilings, ornaments on columns and floors, and
the lighting all combine together
to show a nice harmony. Southern flowers such as dogwood,
magnolia, and Camellia are used
for floor pattern motifs. It dis-
plays southern elegance.

11

**PHIPPS PLAZA FACT SHEET**

Address : 3500 Peachtree Road, NE Atlanta,
Georgia
Developer/Owner : Equitable Real Estate
Investment Management Inc.
Architect/Design : Thompson, Ventullet, Stain-
back & Associates, Inc.
Type : Regional
New/Renovation/Expansion : Phase1/New,
Phase2/Renovation, Expansion
Completion Date : Phase1/1969, Phase2/1992
Gross Size of Center : 48,122m²(Phase1),
99,403m²(Phase2)
Gross Leasable Area : 37,253m²(Phase1),
78,686m²(Phase2)
Number of Parking Space : 2,013(Phase1)
4,150(Phase2)
Anchor/Key Tenant : Saks Fifth Avenue,Lord &
Taylor ,Parisian

12

13

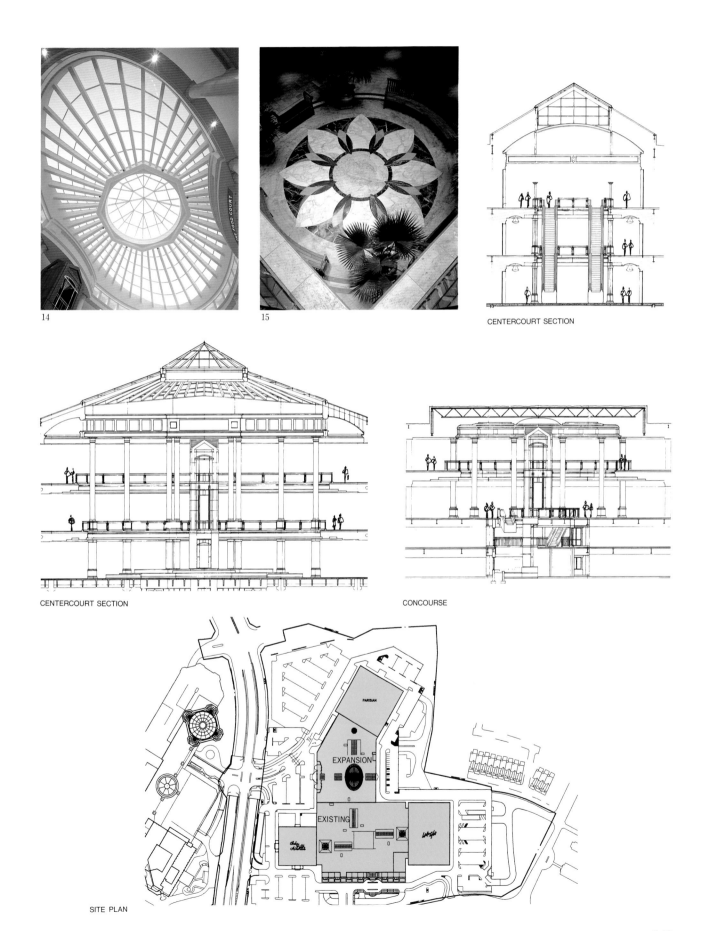

14

15

CENTERCOURT SECTION

CENTERCOURT SECTION

CONCOURSE

SITE PLAN

16. Graphical Wall
17. Entrance
18. Lobby
19. Display Shelf

16

## NIKE TOWN

This is the forefront of Nike stores. The first store was a shop and showroom in Portland, Oregon. The interior of the store stimulates the visitors' athletic side. It is a specially designed environment. This Atlanta shop uses the same concepts which are based on entertaining the visitor. The colors and graphics express the dynamism of athletes and convey the company's image.

17

19

18

# NORTH POINT MALL

## ARCHITECT : ELBASANI & LOGAN ARCHITECTS

Alpharetta , Georgia

1

2

1. Main Entrance
2. Facade
3. View of Food Court
4. Food Court
5. Carousel
6. Patio

3

4

5

6

NORTH·POINT
*Mall*

7

8

"Retaining the old glory of the south and withstanding the hi-tech 21st century" is the concept developed by ELS. Due to the vast number of malls and chain stores, shopping centers are loosing identity. Design will determine shoppers where to go. In designing malls, emphasis is paid to visibility, cleanliness, open space, brightness and elegance. At Northpoint, the romantic historical heritage of the old south is harmonized with contemporary design elements to match the changing hi-tech environment. The conservatory style building was constructed on 12.1 hectare site at $25 million. The roof is suspended by nineteen, 25 meter high masts. Daytime light comes through various skylights and windows. Nighttime illumination is created by reflecting artificial light off the ceiling panels. Corridors are purposely broken at three locations. At each broken corner are skylit courtyards, West Court, East Court and Food Court. Escalators and elevators are see-through and the counter weights are sculpted to be like moving ornaments.

7. Logo
8. Elevator
9. View of Food Court

9

10. View of Mall
11. View of West Court

10

11

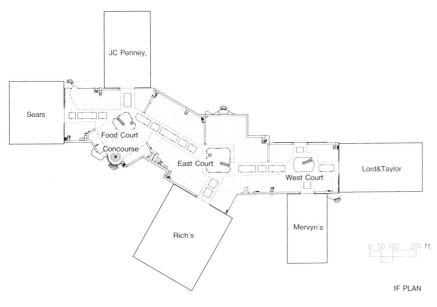

1F PLAN

## NORTH POINT MALL FACT SHEET

Address : 1000 North Point Circle, Alpharetta, GA 30202

Developer/Owner : North Point Mall Limited Partnership

General Partner : North Atlanta Venture Inc. / Homart

Limited Partner : JMB Retail Properties Co.

Architect/Interior Design : ELS/Elbasani & Logan Architects, Berkeley, CA

Completion Date : October 1993

Type : Regional

Total Area of Site : 121,000m$^2$

Department Area : 47,340m$^2$

Gross Leasable Area : 37,200m$^2$

Food Court Area : 3,640m$^2$

Trade Area Population : 1.1 Million

Number of Parking Space : 5,228

Anchor/Key Tenant : Rich's, Sears, JC Penney, Lord & Taylor, Mervyn's,

Photos : Timothy Hursley

12. Atrium at Rich's Departmentstore
13. Cosmetic Counter
14. Childrens Wear Counter

12

## Rich's Department Store

Other stores designed during the 80's were becoming outdated. In Alpharetta, it was important to capture the hearts of mid-30s, middle to upper middle class clients. While retaining the Atlanta store's rich past identity, Alpharetta Rich's was reborn. Four symbolic, silver clocks have been replicated. Arched ceiling and Toscane columns used in other stores have been scaled down to a more friendly size. Skylit, 2100 sq. meter atrium adorns the core sales area.

RICH'S DEPARTMENTSTORE FACT SHEET
Developer／Owner : Federated Department Store Inc.
Interior Design : FRCH Design World Wide
Architect : Cooper Carry & Associates
Photos : Peter Paige

13

14

# MIZNER PARK

## ARCHITECT : COOPER CARRY & ASSOCIATES

Boca Raton, Florida

1

2

3

1. Facade
2. Detail of Facade
3. Spanish Decoration
4. Facade
5. Facade

## Location and Market

This shopping complex is right near the sea. A hundred fifty thousand people reside within a eight kilometer radius of this site and over 480,000 live in a sixteen kilometer radius. From the 1980s and 1990s, the population had grown over 40 percent. During the 1970s, a suburban residential community with golf courses was developed in that area. It attracted many people who adore the Southern Florida lifestyle. Boca Raton is an ideal place for people who enjoy this kind of elegant lifestyle. Most of the residents have high incomes of about $60,000 per year, which is two times higher than the standard income in North America. These people needed a convenient place for shopping. A five minute drive from Mizner Park takes one to the Town Center shopping center which targets high income customers. It has famous departmentstores like Bloomingdale's, Saks Fifth Avenue, and Lord & Taylor.

Mizner Park is designed to get back a flow of shoppers from suburban shopping centers into the downtown area instead.

4

5

154

6. View of Plaza
7. View of Promenade
8. View of Plaza
9. Gazzebo

6

7

8

9

## Development Planning Design

In 1982, the city of Boca Raton established a local development bureau and it started a plan to build a series of facilities at the center of town where people can work, live, and enjoy themselves. This was intended to be a remedy to return local people back downtown. The city government commissioned the project with a developing company. The design concept is " a village in a town " which is provided images of a traditional downtown setting for local people to relax. It consists of European plazas on both ends of two straight roads. The north end of the plaza is a city park with an outdoor theater. The south end is a culture and entertainment center.

The most important element of the planning concept was to deal with the relationship between existing streets and with the project. They also had to express the local color and had to give an identity to the center itself. In the 1920s, Spanish style villas were built in Palm Beach and Boca Raton for the east coast people. Addison Mizner is recognized as a Renaissance man who built those country houses and created the villa style. This project uses the Mizner style, as the project name indicates, to express the local color. The focal point is a fountain in the center of the plaza with several palm trees surrounding it.

10

10. Logo
11. Storefront
12. Directory
13. Shopping Arcade

11

12

13

14. Storefront
15. Site Plan
16. Concept Sketch

14

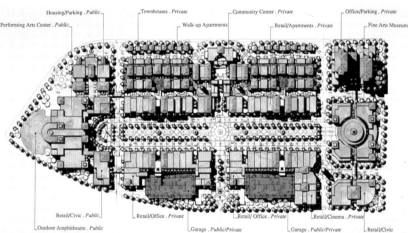

15

The fountain, a gazebo, and colorful flowers gives the visitor a place to take a rest. All four of the major buildings have different heights. The main colors of the buildings are pink, peach and white which is used for the framing. The colors make a good contrast with blue Florida sky and gives the shopper the true feeling of Florida. The entrance to the business district is recessed and there is a small plaza. The arch entrance has silhouetted logo of Mizner Park. A modernized Spanish style helped accentuate the buildings. The windows of an apartment and office building were transformed and given elegant handrails. Facing the plaza, there are shops on the first floor in an arcade to escape from the strong Florida sunshine.

16

**MIZNER PARK FACT SHEET**
Address : 318-400 N, Federal HWY, Boca Raton, Florida
Developer : Crocker & Company
Architect : Cooper Carry & Associates
Type : Community
Completion Date : 1991, Phase2/1994
Gross Size of Center : 21,924m$^2$
Trade Area Population : 150,000
Photos : Stephen Traves, Taguchi Design

# BROWARD MALL

## ARCHITECT : FRCH DESIGN WORLD WIDE

Plantation, Florida

1

2

3

4

1. Main Entrance
2. Main Entrance at Night
3. Sub Entrance
4. Column
5. Food Court Entrance
6. Signboard

5

Located between Miami and Boca Raton, the up-scale resort city of Fort Lauderdale is home to the " Venice of America ". Broward Mall is a ten minute drive from Fort Lauderdale, which is the center of action in the developing South Florida. The design is based on a Mediterranean style. Each entrance to the mall uses Moorish style stucco which was fashionable in the early 20th century in Florida. Particularly impressive was the symbolic main entrance. Six plazas in the mall have fountains. The floors of the plazas are decorated with mosaic to break out of a typical pattern. The most carefully renovated part of the mall was the ceiling. It now has skylights, a pyramid roof covering the central part, and louvers which cast interesting patterns onto the floor.

6

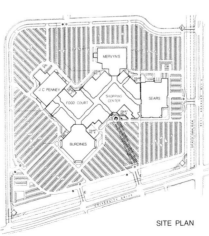

SITE PLAN

### BROWARD MALL FACT SHEET

Address : 8000 West Broward Blvd., Plantation, Florida

Developer : JMB Retail Properties Co.

Architect : FRCH Design World Wide(Renovation)

Completion Date : 1978, Renovation/April 1994

Gross Size of Center : 102,910m²

Trade Area Population : 520,000

Anchor/Key Tenant : Burdines, Mervyn's, JC Penney, Sears

Photos : FRCH Design World Wide, Taguchi Design

7. Main Court
8. Passageway
9. Passageway

7

8

9

# BRANDON TOWNCENTER
## ARCHITECT : RTKL ASSOCIATES

Brandon, Florida

1

2

3

1. Main Entrance
2. Primary Signboard
3. Sub Entrance
4. Facade
5. Food Court Entrance

4

5

6. Entrance
7. Wall Signboard
8. 9. Animal Sculpture

6

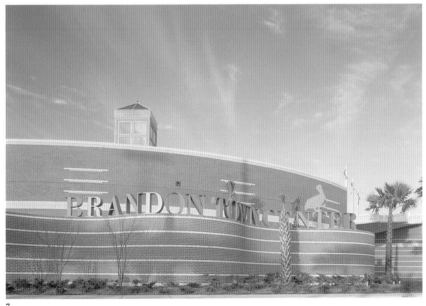

7

8

9

## Location

Tampa, Florida as of 1994 has a population of 290,000. Brandon is a twenty minute drive from downtown. Although Tampa's economic growth is slow, Brandon's is growing rapidly. In this town, the Brandon Town Center opened in February 1995, for the first shopping center in twenty years. It is a very new shopping center to appeal to the customer. The mall targets over 100,000 families whose average income was $36,764 in 1993. The town center is near the highway and easily accessed from downtown. The location is the best that this mall could ask for.

## Project Concept

The Brandon Town Center is a full-scale shopping center. It was designed for those residents who used to have to drive over 25 kilometers to reach a large shopping center. It was designed not only to serve as a shopping center, but also as a community center with an enjoyable and friendly atmosphere. The shopping center is a single story building. The main entrance is located at the center. When the customer enters the center court, she sees Dillard's and JC Penney on the left and Sears and Burdines to her right. There is a line of 120 shops on a 540 meter stretch. The image of the shopping center was based on forests, farm yards, a white church stee-

163

10. View of Mall
11. Rest Area
12. Public Area
13. View of Center Court
14. View of Center Court
15. 16. Lighting Fixture

10

11

12

13

14

15

16

ple, a brick house, and other related structures to create the feeling of the community. The brick facade and the five and seven level towers give the character of a shopping center. Four towers are located on the cross sections to the departmentstores and also on both sides of the center court. The biggest tower is a food court with 536 seats. The interior of the building actually conveys the image of the exterior with an arch ceiling, a round plaza around the tower, and many skylights. Public space occupies eighteen percent of the total site, to focus on the gathering place of the community. There is also a round food court next to the center court that can be accessed through the parking lot. The food court has an open ceiling under one of the tallest towers. It is focal point and a place for dining as well as taking a break. The design motifs are taken from images of frogs, alligators, lizards, manatees, and pelicans which are very popular in Florida. Many local colors are also used as part of the decorations. Fountains, signs, exposed structures are decorated by cute realistic models of the animals. The lot area is 1,052,000 square meters.

17. Food Court
18. Restaurants at Food Court
19. Signboard at Food Court
20. Center Court and Stores
21. Storefront

17

18

19

20

Landscape architects beautifully arranged the trees and brushes that lie around the building and parking lot. The sprinkler system is computerized, making it capable of changing with the weather.

21

**BRANDON TOWNCENTER FACT SHEET**

Address : Brandon, Florida
Owner/Developer : JMB Retail Properties Co.
Architect : RTKL Associates/Baltimore
Type : Regional
Completion Date : February 1995
Gross Size of Center : 90,485m²
Number of Parking Space : 5,000
Anchor/Key Tenant : Dillard's, JC Penney, Burdines, Sears
Photos : David Whitcomb, Taguchi Design

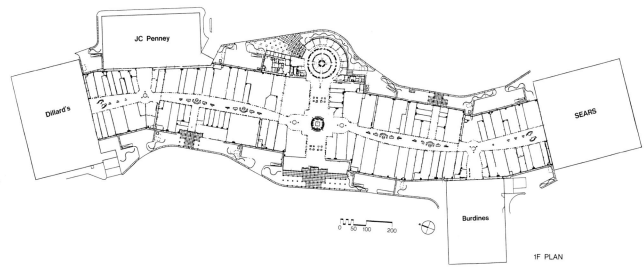

JC Penney

Dillard's

SEARS

Burdines

0 50 100    200

1F PLAN

22. Flog's Sculpture
23. Lizard's Sculpture
24. Foot of Tower
25. Graphic Design
26. 27. 28. Animal's Sculpture
29. Directory

22

23

24

25

26

27

28

29

# UNIVERSITY MALL

## ARCHITECT : ANTHONY BELLUSCHI ARCHITECTS

Tampa, Florida

1

2

1. Entrance at Night
2. Entrance
3. Side Court/West Side
4. Side Court/East Side
5. Wave Pattern and Fishes
6. Center Court

## Project Concept and Design

Twenty years after opening, a super regional center was renovated to reestablish a major shopping mall in this area. Parts of the facade, the interior, and public space were renewed to create a new and exciting atmosphere and visual effect for the shopping center. The shopping center followed a traditional tenants-mix when in 1983, a fifth anchor tenant was added. The building stands along a road from which one can notice the anchor tenants on both edges of the center. It is a single storied structure with a simple floor plan. An easy, attractive, and low budget way of giving a outdated shopping center a face lift, is redesigning signs, entrances, and public space. The environmental graphic design program is an important strategy in such situations. The renovation project of University Mall uses this strategy to clean up its total image. Florida's symbols of the sun, the moon, and the sea are all used as design motifs for the shopping center. A new logo was developed to represent the sun.

3

4

5

6

7. Sidewalk
8. Signboard
9. Site Plan

Other graphic works include new signs, ads, and pamphlets. The main entrance is shaped in a half circle with a trellis around it. The half circle has the new logo and beacon-like towers with white columns as a symbolic sign for the whole structure. The main entrance is beautifully lit up at night.

7

8

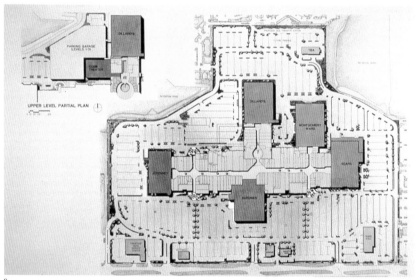

9

**UNIVERSITY MALL FACT SHEET**

Address : Tampa, Florida
Developer : Heitman Retail Properties
Architect : Anthony Belluschi Architects
Environment Graphic Design : FRCH World Wide Design
Type : Super Regional
Completion Date : 1974, Renovation/November 1993, Phase2/October 1996
Gross Size of Center : 107,764m²
Anchor/Key Tenant : Dillard's Burdines, Sears, JC Penney, Montgomery Ward
Photos : George Cott, Chroma Inc., Taguchi Design

# MAIN STREET

## ARCHITECT : PALMER BROOK SCHOOLEY

Houston, Texas

1

2

3

1. Facade

2. 3. Facade Sketch

4. Complete View

5. Corner of Facade

6. Promenade

7. Storefront

4

5

6

7

Almost every American town has its own main street at one point in its history. This important street in the center of town is where retail stores, offices, restaurants, and various fun places were built. It is also this place where local people meet with friends, and do all kinds of errands.

Since the 1950s, rapid decline of the inner city had sometimes led to the changing of the main streets. The main streets have given the developers attractive concepts for the shopping center which creates vitalities of the old times.

The Kingscrossing community, a large scale residential development is a forty minute drive from Houston, Texas. The main street of this commercial complex is a good example of a recreation of an old main street image. Including the people of the adjacent town, the population of this area is about 80,000.

The town center was developed as a new type of complex with a beautiful natural environment surrounding it.

The main street is accessible by cars, but is geared more toward the pedestrian. The small shops give the homey, human scale attention and atmosphere. Regulations were set on the heights of buildings, set-back, density of parking lot, and the building materials. However, flexibilities on regulations allow each build-

8. 9. Facade
10. Alley
11. Site Plan

ing to be designed individually. The project is designed based on a main street of a small town in Texas in the late 19th or the early 20th century style.

A balcony and an arcade were built for the store front as an enjoyable place for the customers to walk. The focal point, a clock tower at one corner of the building, faces a park.

The exterior wall is made of stucco and brick. They work well to show the main street images. The brick work uses a traditional patterns and has a simple look. The columns and walls are designed to express the contrast effect of light and shadow of the hot Texas sunshine. Green was used as the finishing touches on metallic parts. As a whole, the mall shows us a small modernized main street of an old town.

8

9

10

**MAIN STREET FACT SHEET**

Address : Kingwood, Houston, Texas
Developer : KCTC Inc., J. Ty Eckley
Architect : Palmer Brook Schooley
Type : Neighborhood
Completion Date : October 1994, Phase2/October 1995
Gross Size of Center : Phase1/2,136m², Phase2/2,972m²
Photos : Gerald Moorhead

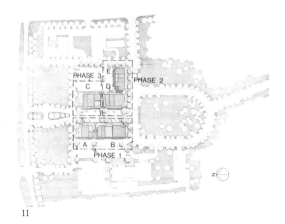

11

176

# LOEHMANN'S FASHION ISLAND
## ARCHITECT : JOHN R. DEBELLO ARCHITECT

Aventura, Florida

1

2

3

1. Entry Structure
2. Entrance
3. Rest Area at Entry Structure
4. Stores
5. Outdoor Cafe
6. View of Mall

Loehmann's Fashion Island is situated on Aventura, Florida between Miami and Fort Lauderdale. The site was originally a swampy and damp region. Since the 1970s, it has been rapidly developed to become a growing residential area in southern Florida. Aventura is still developing with high income residential areas of big companies, yacht clubs, marinas, with Tunberry Resort Isle as its core.

**Project Concept and Design**
PCT Biscayne Boulevard Partnership, a new owner of the mall, analyzed the building from various aspects. They concluded that a shopping center in this district for high income bracket shoppers should not be geared toward be discount-oriented.

The commercial tactics are selecting appropriate merchandise for the regional market and developing an agreeable shopping environment for local customers.

It has an eight screened AMC theater and Loehmann's, a discount store of famous brands and designer's clothing, as anchor tenants. This mall is also used as a meeting and gathering place for the local people. Specialty stores were to be allocated around the anchor stores. Considering the project's budget, the final plan of redevelopment was based on leaving as much of the original part of the building as

4

5

6

7. Facade
8. Fountain
9. Storefront
10. Awning

7

8

9

10

11. Super Market
12. Corner of Facade
13. Signboard
14. Environmental Graphic

11

12

possible. It is designed as an open air shopping center. It has many courtyards, garden style promenades, and refreshing fountains around it to create an oasis type environment. The architectural style and total image of the mall is based upon a classical Caribbean style. A two-story building was annexed to create a visual connection from the parking lot to the shopping center. The building windows have half opened shades and flower pots under that relay a friendly image to the shoppers. The twelve meter high trellis-like mall gate on the main street is covered with bougainvilleas and it looks very charming and attractive to anyone who passes or drives by.

13

14

**LOEHMANN'S FASHION ISLAND FACT SHEET**
Address : Aventura, Florida
Owner : PCT Biscayne Boulevard Partnership
Architect : John R. DeBello Architect
Completion Date (Renovation) : Spring 1994
Gross Size of Center : 26,012 m²
Anchor/Key Tenant : Loehmann's, Barnes & Noble, AMC Theater
Photos : Sue Hoyt, Taguchi Design

# PEMBROKE LAKES MALL

## ARCHITECT : SPILLIS CANDELA & PARTNERS

Pembroke Pines, Florida

1

2

3

1. Main Entrance at Night
2. Burdines Entrance
3. Facade
4. View of Glass Dome
5. View of Glass Dome

4

5

Pembroke Lakes Mall is located north of Miami (a one-hour drive). It is situated where there was no shopping center within a trade radius of about 14 km before, despite the rapid increase of population since 1980. Pembroke opened as a super-regional shopping center with five anchor tenants to serve a young family marketplace in an area where there is strong growth of such population.

This area has been developed along with new roads, for a town without a city center. So the mall was designed to be a communal center like the old town square. The primary design goal was to create an environment for pedestrian activity where people can get together and enjoy themselves. The mall was architecturally designed in the Mediterranean style, meant to bring back the experience and the fantasy that was a part of the architectural period. The mall utilizes the flat topography on a long site and provides a picturesque entry experience with two bell towers.

### PEMBROKE LAKES MALL FACT SHEET
Address : Pembroke Pines, Florida
Owner/Developer : Homart, The Edward J. DeBartolo Corp.
Architect : Spillis Candela & Partners Inc.
Type : Super Regional
Completion Date : Spring 1992, Expansion/ Spring 1995
Gross Size of Center : 101,000m²
Anchor/Key Tenant : Dillard's, Mervyn's, Burdines, JC Penney, Sears
Photos : Dan Fover, Taguchi Design

6. View of Mall

7. View of Mall

8. Food Court

6

7

8

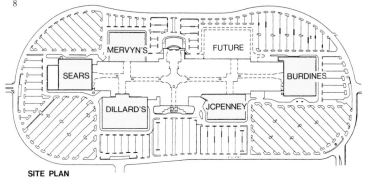

SITE PLAN

# AMERICA'S NEW FOOD COURT
## As an Anchor for Shopping Center

TADASHI HIROMOTO

### Food Court as an Oasis for Shoppers

The American way of life has changed, and in turn changed the American shopping habits and preferences. "Couch potato" and "cocooning" are not just trendy terms, but an integral part of the American lifestyle of the 1990's. Recession pressures shoppers to search for consumer goods at lower prices. The average American woman has less leisure shopping time, as she spends more time in the workforce, as her male counterparts. Americans want to spend more time in sports, traveling and other leisure activities.

Under these circumstances, shopping centers are changing their style. Factory outlets and power centers, equipped with specialty shops and discount prices are in fashion. Traditional shopping centers are trying to survive the onslaught of competition. Modern consumers want to finish shopping in as soon as possible. 48% of them consider shopping to be "painful" rather than "joyful".

How can the traditional malls regain the consumers whose mottoes are "quick", "easy" and "simple"? People want to spend less, and be entertained at the same time. They are attracted to centers which can provide both. Recently, over 40 various size shopping centers have opened in the metropolitan New York area. None of them were "regional" shopping centers.

They consisted of "strip malls", super markets, home centers and neighborhood discount stores. They are convenient shopping centers where customers can get their shopping done quickly as possible.

On the other hand, there are healthy traditional large scale shopping centers that have kept up with the changes. One such example is the 500,000 square meter Bridgewater Commons Shopping Center in Sommerset, New Jersey.

Its renovations have followed the important themes of providing a comfortable environment, and ample food court in order to

1. Bridge Water Comons
2. Garden State Plaza
3. Gurnee Mills
4. Newport Bearch Fashion Island
5. Citadel Factory Outlet Collection

3

make shopping painless and fun. The new exterior gets rid of cold' materials such as concrete. The interior images the feel of the park and forest. The parking lot is also surrounded by a large amount of trees. Architect Chan has succeeded in giving each shop individuality, yet maintain the harmony as a whole. The renovated food court serves as an oasis, and results in shoppers staying longer.

To set itself apart from smaller malls, large shopping centers provide large open spaces in the form of atriums and gallerias. Well designed food court plays an important role in attracting and raising customer's per capita spending.

Super regional Delmore Fashion Center in the suburb of Los Angeles boasts 270,000 square meters of retail area, 371 stores and 12,000 car parking.

Tenants vary from fashionable boutiques, department stores to discount stores. Generally speaking, high-end fashion shops could not co-exist with discount shops under the same roof. This concept is eroding. Consumers enjoy variety as long as the layout is clear. After addition and renovation in 1981 and 1987, Delmore now boasts a 15 screen movie theater and the second largest food court in the USA (largest being the Ala Moana Center, Hawaii).

Facing Manhattan, across the Hudson river is the state of New Jersey which has a high density daytime population. Conversely, there is a high density of shopping centers, such as Garden State Plaza, Palms Park, The Fashion Center, Riverside Square and Bargain Mall. Unlike in Japan where the ratio of a shopping center to population is 1 : 100,000, the ratio in the USA is 1 : 10,000 (10 times more competitive).

Garden State Plaza originally opened in 1958, has repeatedly renovated itself to satisfy the consumer needs including food court expansion. It also welcomed Nordstrom to open its

4

5

first Northeastern region store.

**Magnetic Power of Food Court**
Newport Beach Fashion Island SC lies 75 kilometers to the south of downtown Los Angeles. It opened in September 1976 with about thirty tenants.

After several renovations, it is known as one of the most beautiful shopping malls. In the last two decades, it is facing stiff competition from neighboring South Court Plaza and other malls. In 1990, Newport Beach Fashion Island went through extensive renovation. A 15,000 square meter atrium was built. A high-end food court was placed on the ground floor, and 60 boutiques on the upper floors. The exterior was modeled after Mediterranean style and the interior now rivals that of New York's Trump Tower and Chicago's 900 North Michigan. With the 165 seat food court and gourmet market, the ground floor now buzz with customers.

Citadel Factory Outlet Collection, opened in November 1990, was the first factory outlet center in the Los Angeles area. Modeled after European shopscape, the layout guides shoppers through colorful shades and stream.

This 50 tenants center added a glass-roofed, seven eatery food court a year later.

Western Development managed giant Mills outlets (Potomac, DC; Franklin, Philadelphia; Sawgrass, Fort Lauderdale; Guernee, Chicago); assures the incorporation of several large food courts in each location.

Recently opened, giant Woodfield Village Green and Bloomingdale's Court in the Chicago area, recognizes the vital drawing power of their food court.

Furthermore, Plaza in Lake Forest, New Orleans, has replaced their skating rink with a food court. Food courts are recognized as a vital magnet for attracting more customers.

6

7

# STATE FARE FOOD COURT

## DESIGNER : SHEA ASSOCIATES

Gavidae Comon

1

2

1. View of Food Court
2. Restaurant AZUR
3. Neon Arcade
4. Corner of Food Court
5. Chairs
6. Restaurant AZUR

3

4

5

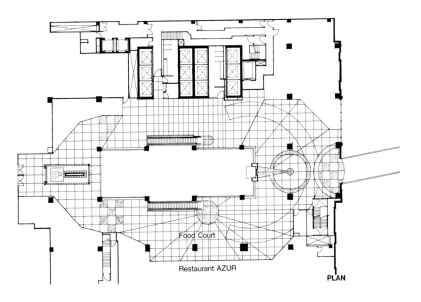

6

This food court is on the fourth floor of an up-scale shopping mall in downtown Minneapolis. This location is chosen to activate the flow of people to pass by all the floors of the mall.

The design concept of the mall is based upon a state bird. The food court is designed to represent the state fair as pride, nostalgia, recreation, and feast.

Lamps blinking on and off, shiny neon lamps, big models of hot dogs, ice cream, peanuts and corn are important design elements to express the joys and history of the state fair. The interior is made livelier by being lit up by big format photos of past state fairs.

**STATE FARE FOOD COURT DATA**
Shopping Center : Gavidae Comon
Address : Gavidae Comon, Minneapolis
Food Court Area : 2,044m²
Photos : SHEA Associates

Food Court

Restaurant AZUR

**PLAN**

# BOULEVARD CAFE
## DESIGNER : RTKL ASSOCIATES

Montgomery Mall

1

2

3

1. View of Food Court
2. Display Counter
3. Signboard
4. View of Food Court
5. View of Food Court
6. Miniature Chef

4

After renovation, Montgomery Mall was built with a new food court which were decorated with joyful moving models. The Cafe Kitchen is visually expressed using a French chef figure as one of the moving models. He is a star of " The Fun Thing " by using this high technology. Every five minutes the chef statue acts like a host and speaks to its guests. There is also a teapot that dances, the chef's dog that barks, and a cat that meows. This food court is able to entertain every generation that visits the food court as if they are visiting a mini theater.

5

**BOULEVARD CAFE DATA**
Shopping Center : Montgomery Mall
Address : Bethesda, Maryland
Food Court Area : 1,858 m²
Number of Sheet : 550
Number of Stores : 12
Photos : David Whitcomb

6

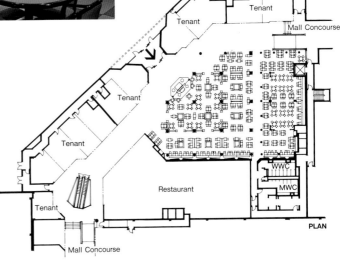

Tenant

Tenant

Mall Concourse

Tenant

Tenant

Tenant

WWC

MWC

Restaurant

Tenant

Mall Concourse

**PLAN**

191

# THE FOOD GARDEN
## DESIGNER : THOMPSON, VENTULETT, STAINBACK & ASSOCIATES

Northlake Mall

1

1. View of Food Court
2. Food Court at Night
3. View of Food Court

2

3

With the renovation and extension, the existing food court inside was moved to the roadside so that the people could find it easier and to make a place for gathering in the local community. The food court is an anchor to emphasize the difference amongst other malls. Either inside or outside of the Food Garden, customers can enjoy a natural environment. It is designed upon a British Covent Garden and greenhouse constructed by steel and glass. There are 500 seats, big glazed windows, a cathedral roof, and a cupola which characterizes the building and lets in a lot of natural light.

## THE FOOD GARDEN DATA
Shopping Center : Northlake Mall
Address : Atlanta, Georgia
Food Court Area : 913m²
Number of Sheet : 500
Photos : Brian Gassel

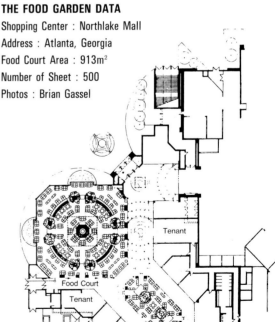

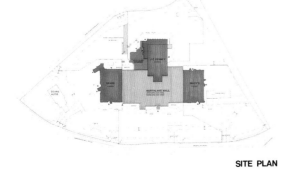

SITE PLAN

PLAN

# THE FESTIVAL

## DESIGNER : MICHAEL SCHUSTER ASSOCIATES

Forest Fair Mall

1

1. View of Food Court
2. Food Court Entrance
3. View of Food Court

2

Entertainment restaurant "Festival" serves as a draw to home-ward bound workers. Malls need the "attraction" to bring in and keep potential shoppers in the center longer. How to achieve this goals is a major task for all mall management. Festival addressed this by opening high end restaurants offering entertainment. Now customers come to the mall, attracted by the food and pleasures of the Festival.

3

**THE FESTIVAL DATA**
Shopping Center : Forest Fair Mall
Address : Fairfield, Ohio
Gross Area of Center : 130,000m²
Food Court Area : 10,380m²
Photos : Ron Forth

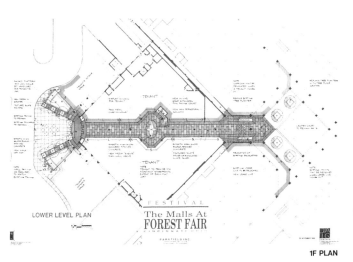

LOWER LEVEL PLAN

1F PLAN

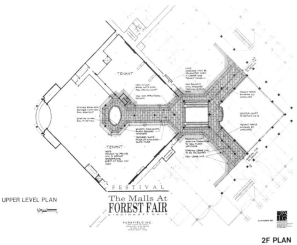

UPPER LEVEL PLAN

2F PLAN

# PANORAMA CAFE
## DESIGNER : RTKL ASSOCIATES

Boulevard Mall

1

2

3

196

1. View of Food Court
2. Main Entrance at Night
3. Food Court Entrance
4. View of Food Court
5. View of Center Court

4

In 1992, Boulevard Mall went through a 60 million dollar renovation. It added rows of palm trees on granite walkways and a fountain. Gold leaf and triangular stainless steel ornaments decorate above the fountain. The 600 seat, 1,860 square meter, oval spaced Panorama Cafe was part of the major renovation. The walls of the cafe is surrounded by a panorama mural of scenes from Hollywood's golden era. It succeeds in creating a unique environment.

5

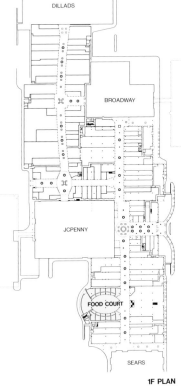

DILLADS

BROADWAY

JCPENNY

FOOD COURT

SEARS

**1F PLAN**

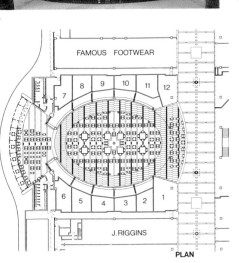

FAMOUS FOOTWEAR

7 8 9 10 11 12

6 5 4 3 2 1

J. RIGGINS

**PLAN**

Tenant List
1. Everything Yougurt & Salad Cafe
2. Orange Julius/Dairy Queen
3. Country Inn Express
4. Fingr's
5. Scully's Bread and Chowder
6. Panda Express
7. Sbarro
8. Hibachi San
9. Great Steak & Potatato Company
10. Flamers Charbroiled Hamburgers
11. La Salsa
12. Cinnabon

**PANORAMA CAFE DATA**

Shopping Center : Boulevard Mall

Address : Boulevard, Las Vegas

Food Court Area : 1,860m²

Number of Sheet : 600

Number of Stores : 12

Photos : Scott McDonald

# METRO FOOD COURT

## DESIGNER : FRCH DESIGN WORLD WIDE

Eaton Center

1

1. View of Food Court
2. View of Food Court
3. Video Monitor Wall

2

3

Metro Town is located in high density area of Vancouver where three shopping centers, two office complexes and a hotel come together. To accommodate lunch hour crowd of this fast growing environment, the food court was expanded by 50%, now 1,000 seats and 3,720 square meters. The challenge was how to expand in a limited and enclosed second floor space. The designer succeeded by installing a multi-screen video wall to light up the interior.

These interactive monitors continuously show news, sport events and other area of the mall.

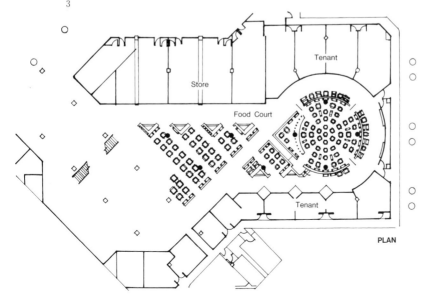

PLAN

**METRO FOOD COURT DATA**
Shopping Center : Eaton Center
Address : Metrotown, Vancouver, Canada
Food Court Area : 3,720m²
Number of Sheet : 1,000

# CORONADO CAFE
### DESIGNER : FRCH DESIGN WORLD WIDE

Coronado Center

1

Coronado Center always ranked high in the most competitive area of New Mexico. The food court was added as a means to keep the customers longer.

The design motif for the 1,860 square meter Coronado Cafe is Southwestern. Indian icons, eagles, geckos, snakes and other local symbols were incorporated to create joyful bright atmosphere.

2

5

**CORONADO CAFE DATA**
Shopping Center : Coronado Center
Address : Albuquerque, New Mexico
Gross Area of Center : 101,500m²
Food Court Area : 1,860m²
Number of Sheet : 325
Number of Stores : 9

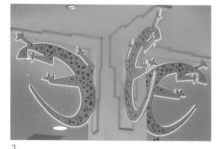

3

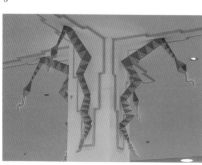

4

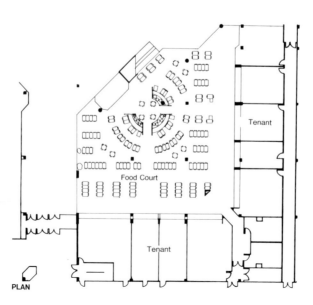

PLAN

1. View of Food Court
2. 3. 4. Object
5. Signboard